Frames of War

JUDITH BUTLER is Maxine Elliot Professor of Rhetoric and Comparative Literature at the University of California, Berkeley. She is the author of many books, including *Giving an Account of Oneself*, *Precarious Life*, and *Gender Trouble*.

Frames of War

When Is Life Grievable?

JUDITH BUTLER

VERSO
London • New York

Firm Amaz 9/10 16.95

This paperback edition first published by Verso 2010
First published by Verso 2009
© Judith Butler 2010
All rights reserved

The moral rights of the author have been asserted

1 3 5 7 9 10 8 6 4 2

Verso
UK: 6 Meard Street, London W1F 0EG
US: 20 Jay Street, Suite 1010, Brooklyn, NY 11201
www.versobooks.com

Verso is the imprint of New Left Books

ISBN-13: 978-1-84467-626-2

British Library Cataloguing in Publication Data
A catalogue record for this book is available from the British Library

Library of Congress Cataloging-in-Publication Data
A catalog record for this book is available from the Library of Congress

Typeset by Hewer Text UK Ltd, Edinburgh
Printed in the US by Maple Vail

Contents

Acknowledgments

These essays were written and revised between 2004 and 2008. Although some of them have appeared in earlier forms, they have been substantially revised for the purposes of this book. An earlier version of Chapter 1, "Survivability, Vulnerability, Affect," was published by the Centre de Cultura Contemporània de Barcelona in English and Catalan in 2008. "Torture and the Ethics of Photography" appeared in an earlier version in *Society and Space*, the journal of the Royal Geographical Society, and in *Bilderpolitik in Zeiten von Krieg und Terror: Medien, Macht und Geschlechterverhältnisse*, ed. Linda Hentschel, Berlin: b_books, 2008. Chapter 2 also draws on my essay "Photography, War, Outrage," published in the *PMLA* in December 2005. "Sexual Politics, Torture, and Secular Time" appeared first in the *British Journal of Sociology* (59: 1) in March 2008. "Non-Thinking in the Name of the Normative" draws upon a reply I wrote to several responses to "Sexual Politics" in the *British Journal of Sociology* (59: 2). "The Claim of Non-Violence" draws upon "Violence and Non-Violence of Norms: Reply to Mills and Jenkins," in *differences* (18: 2) in fall 2007. The argument of the text was elaborated in a series of seminars I gave in

Paris for the École Normale Supérieure and the École des hautes études in the spring of 2008.

I am grateful for discussions I have had with several interlocutors over these last years which informed and changed my thinking: Frances Bartkowski, Étienne Balibar, Jay Bernstein, Wendy Brown, Yoon Sook Cha, Alexandra Chasin, Tom Dumm, Samera Esmeir, Michel Feher, Eric Fassin, Faye Ginsburg, Jody Greene, Amy Huber, Nacira Guénif-Souilamas, Shannon Jackson, Fiona Jenkins, Linda Hentschel, Saba Mahmood, Paola Marrati, Mandy Merck, Catherine Mills, Ramona Naddaff, Denise Riley, Leticia Sabsay, Gayle Salamon, Kim Sang Ong-Van-Cung, Joan W. Scott, Kaja Silverman, and Linda Williams. I am grateful for the Humanities Research Fellowship at the University of California at Berkeley and Dean Janet Broughton who provided me with the support required to finish this text. I thank Colleen Pearl and Jill Stauffer for their editorial work on the manuscript (though all errors are emphatically mine). I thank Tom Penn at Verso for encouraging and editing the project. The text is dedicated to my students who have moved and changed my thinking.

This manuscript was completed a month after the election of Barack Obama to the US presidency, and we have yet to see what concrete ameliorations of war may take place under his administration. In a way, the occasions for these essays emerged from the wars instigated by the Bush administration, but I am clear that the reflections contained herein are not limited to the vagaries of that regime. The critique of war emerges from the occasions of war, but its aim is to rethink the complex and fragile character of the social bond and to consider what conditions might make violence less possible, lives more equally grievable, and, hence, more livable.

Introduction to the Paperback Edition

This volume gathers a set of essays that return in different ways to common themes. There is no single argument here, but rather a series of forays into thinking about the ways in which visual and discursive fields are part of war recruitment and war waging. The point is not merely descriptive, but critical and oppositional. After all, there are conditions under which war is waged, and we have to know them if we are to oppose war. Indeed, the opposition to war has to take place, in part, through remaking the conditions of its possibility and probability. Similarly, if war is to be opposed, we have to understand how popular assent to war is cultivated and maintained, in other words, how war waging acts upon the senses so that war is thought to be an inevitability, something good, or even a source of moral satisfaction.

Any effort to understand must consider how wars are waged and the technology of war, but to understand the operation of technology we have to consider how it works on the field of the senses. What is formed and framed through the technological grasp and circulation of the visual and discursive dimensions of war? This grasping and circulation is already an interpretive maneuver, a way of giving an account of whose life *is* a life, and whose life is effectively transformed into an instrument, a target, or a number, or is effaced with only a trace remaining or none at all. Although no final or exhaustive account of war waging is undertaken in these pages, some suggestions are made about what form such an account might take. Such a task requires that we rethink the received terms of materialism in order to understand, for instance, how cameras work as instruments of war, how they both frame and form the human and non-human target along with a field of collateral damage (equally necessary to war, even if perpetually part of peripheral vision), and to develop an anti-war politics that focuses on the dispossessed and those rendered precarious in ways that require new vocabularies and new practices.

When we think about how wars are waged, what forms war waging takes, we tend to think first about the material instruments of war, assuming that we know what we mean by "material instruments" when we speak this way. Even if we agree that cameras are among the material instruments of war, it remains understandably difficult to say that the cameras themselves wage war, or even that they are part of war waging. Surely, common sense tells us that persons wage war, not the instruments they employ. But what happens if the instruments acquire their own agency, such that persons become extensions of those instruments? The populations targeted can be cast as instruments of war, as happened most recently in the effort to justify civilian deaths caused by the Israeli army in Gaza. Similarly, the soldier can be treated as an extension of the instrument he carries, when the soldier is considered one with the weapon he bears, but so too can the camera sometimes appear to be co-extensive with the camera's use. When cast as a mere instrument of aggressive military power, a threat to civilization, or as a potentially unmanageable demographic problem, populations are framed by the tactics of war, and living humans become cast as instruments, blockades, targets and shields. Similarly, very often the one who uses the camera is positioned within the perspective of battle, and becomes a soldier-reporter who visually consecrates the destructive acts of war. As a result, we have to pose the question of the material of war waging, what counts as material, and whether cameras and their images are part of that extended materiality.

Although we reserve some sense of materiality for the image, we tend to give priority to that materiality that belongs to guns, bombs, and the directly destructive instruments of war without realizing that they cannot operate without the image.[1] In a way, that focusing on the target produces a position for the soldier, the reporter, and the public audience, structuring the visual field that makes each position possible. The frame not only orchestrates such positions, but also delimits the visual field itself. In the context of war photography, the image may reflect or document a war; at times it may rally emotional responses either in support of the war effort or in resistance to it. Other times the image becomes a dense site of political ambivalence about the war itself. So can we say that the image itself is really part of the waging of war? Cameras are literally appended to missiles and bombing devices, sometimes replacing human agency—as with the pilot-less drones whose destructiveness in the war in Afghanistan cannot be doubted. Indeed, the camera-bomber that is the drone has produced many civilian casualties, since its aim is imprecise and its destructive power always disproportionate to its target.

Efforts to control the visual and narrative dimensions of war delimit public discourse by establishing and disposing the sensuous parameters of reality itself—including what can be seen and what can be heard. As a result, it makes sense to ask, does regulating the limits of what is visible or

---

1 For an excellent visual exploration of the relation between human and machine in the mapping of military targets, see these videos by Harun Farocki: "Eye Machine, I, II, III" (2001–3) and "War at a Distance" (2003).

audible serve as a precondition of war waging, one facilitated by cameras and other technologies of communication? Of course, persons use technological instruments, but instruments surely also use persons (position them, endow them with perspective, and establish the trajectory of their action); they frame and form anyone who enters into the visual or audible field, and, accordingly, those who do not. But further, under conditions of war waging, personhood is itself cast as a kind of instrumentality, by turns useful or dispensable. How is the public sphere constituted by the visual technologies of war? And what counter-public emerges over and against that ideal postulate? We think of persons as reacting to war in various ways, but communicable reactions to war also variably constitute and de-constitute personhood within the field of war. Is there some way to register war in a way that transforms the senses? And what role do transformed senses have in the demands for the cessation of war? If those of us who watch the wars our governments conduct at a distance are visually solicited and recruited into the war by embedded reporting and publicly approved media reports, under what conditions can we refuse that recruitment effort? What restructuring of the senses does that require and enable?

To approach this question, we have to understand how the senses are part of any recruitment effort. Specifically, there is a question of the epistemological position to which we are recruited when we watch or listen to war reports. Further, a certain reality is being built through our very act of passive reception, since what we are being recruited into is a certain framing of reality, both its constriction and its interpretation. When the state issues directives on how war is to be reported, indeed on whether war is to be reported at all, it seems to be trying to regulate the understanding of violence, or the appearance of violence within a public sphere which has become decisively transformed by the internet and other forms of digital media. But if we are to ask whether this regulation of violence is itself also violent in some way, part of violence, then we need a more careful vocabulary to distinguish between the destruction of the bomb and the framing of its reality, even though, as we know, both happen at the same time, and the one cannot happen without the other. In the same way that Althusser (drawing on Spinoza) once argued that there can be different modalities of materiality, there can surely be, and are, different modalities of violence and of the material instrumentalities of violence. How do we understand the frame as itself part of the materiality of war and the efficacy of its violence?

The frame does not simply exhibit reality, but actively participates in a strategy of containment, selectively producing and enforcing what will count as reality. It tries to do this, and its efforts are a powerful wager. Although framing cannot always contain what it seeks to make visible or readable, it remains structured by the aim of instrumentalizing certain versions of reality. This means that the frame is always throwing something away, always keeping something out, always de-realizing and de-legitimating alternative versions of reality, discarded negatives of the official version. And so, when the frame jettisons certain versions of war, it is busily making a rubbish heap whose animated debris provides the potential resources for resistance. When versions of reality are excluded or jettisoned to a domain of unreality, then specters are produced that haunt the ratified version of reality, animated and de-ratifying traces. In this sense frame seeks to institute an interdiction on mourning: there is no destruction, and there is no loss. Even as the frames are actively engaged in redoubling the destruction of war, they are only polishing the surface of a melancholia whose rage must be contained, and often cannot. Although the frame initiates (as part of weaponry) or finishes off (as part of reporting) a whole set of murderous deeds, and seeks to subordinate the visual field to the task of war waging, its success depends upon a successful conscription of the public. Our responsibility to resist war depends in part on how well we resist that daily effort at conscription.

We may think that circulating alternative images will rally resistance, but we have to remember that graphic depictions can sometimes do no more than sensationalize events. When that happens, we respond with outrage periodically, but the outrage is not transformed into a sustained political resistance. Is there another way to act upon the senses, or to act from them, that resists both sensationalism and episodic outrage at the limits on the visual imposed by techniques of war waging?

The image is nearly impossible to control by virtue of the contemporary forms of its reproducibility and circulability. But this uncontrollability is not a sufficient basis for utopian excitement. Images within digital culture travel beyond the reach of those who seek to censor them and sometimes run counter to whatever intentions animate them at the start. Circulation reanimates intentions in new ways, exposes the image to new animating conditions, and often ends up producing effects that turn back on those whose control is supposed to be reflected back and solidified through the circulation itself.[2] This was one effect of the frenzied circulation of the Abu Ghraib photos on the internet. Indeed, the uncontrolled circulability of the image and shifting contexts of its reception helped to produce a public outcry against the war across the globe.

On the other hand, that same uncontrolled circulability can work to scatter the effects of war, undermine our ability to focus on its costs, and even naturalize the effects of war as a presupposed background of everyday life. This is a consequential metalepsis when the visual effects of war become the ground of everyday life. The destruction of our

---

2 See W. J. T. Mitchell, *Cloning Terror: The War of Images, 9/11 to the Present*, Chicago: University of Chicago Press, forthcoming 2011.

ability to focus is yet another form of collateral damage. As a result, intensified circulability cannot be affirmed as an unequivocal utopian effect of new visual technology, since the transmutation of ordinary life into the continuation of war is a clear and present risk.

Indeed, we must ask: can there be the continuation of war or, indeed, the escalation of war, as we are now witnessing in Afghanistan, without first preparing and structuring the public understanding of what war is, and by attempting to suppress any visual, audible, or narrative accounts of war that might help to break open a popular resistance to war? Television coverage of war positions citizens as visual consumers of a violent conflict that happens elsewhere, at least in the United States where geographical distance from our so-called enemies allows us to wage war without close domestic scrutiny of our actions. It may be that global media operations like CNN actually export the perspective of the US, enforcing a sense of infinite distance from zones of war even for those who live in the midst of violence. But if the framing of what we see challenges the credibility of the claims made about war, then we fail to be effectively recruited into the war effort by the news. Indeed, if soldiers fail to be interpellated by the visual and narrative accounts of the wars they fight, then they start to lose faith in what they do, claim to be ill, go AWOL, request a transfer, stop working, or simply leave. The incentives to do this are not great, especially when soldiers are recruited with the promise of escaping poverty and acquiring job skills. In this way, they become instruments of the economy and begin in neo-liberal fashion to calculate their chances at success rather than ask whether the war is just or justified. It does not help that the discourse of justification has been effectively subordinated to strategic aims, at which point there is no operative public way to distinguish between instrumental forms of reasoning and normative justifications. To achieve a normative evaluation of a war, we have first to be able to take it in, to register war by

the senses in ways that allow us openly and publicly to
question whether such destruction is justifiable.

In some sense, every war is a war upon the senses,
which does not mean that, conversely, only the senses can
save us now. There is no thinking and judgment without
the senses, and there is no thinking and judgment about
war without the senses assuming a social form that can
be reliably reproduced over time. The assault can take
various forms: rendering sensational losses that are borne
by nations with whom identification is intensified through
the individual icons of death, rendering insensate certain
losses whose open mourning might challenge the rationale
of war itself. Without the assault on the senses, it would
be impossible for a state to wage war. Waging war in some
ways begins with the assault on the senses; the senses are
the first target of war. Similarly, the implicit or explicit
framing of a population as a war target is the initial action
of destruction. It is not just preparation for a destruction
to come, but the initiating sequence of the process of
destruction.

Shall we perhaps expand our idea of how wars are waged
in order to understand how the regulation of the visible
and audible field seeks to maintain the apparent public
consensus that permits a state to wage its wars without
instigating a popular revolt?

Although the images of war are meant to recruit us
to the waging of war, they also solicit us in other ways.
Even when the precarious condition of targeted lives
is precisely what we are not supposed to see, we can
nevertheless apprehend that precarity at the limit of the
frame. The apprehension of the precarity of others—their
exposure to violence, their socially induced transience and
dispensability—is, by implication, an apprehension of the
precarity of any and all living beings, implying a principle
of equal vulnerability that governs all living beings. Since
we are also living, the apprehension of another's precarity
is implicitly an apprehension of our own, although the

singular determination of lives makes it impossible to assimilate the one into the other. In other words, equal vulnerability does not imply radical substitutability; and yet, formally, there is no living being that is not at risk of destruction. At the same time, precarity is distributed unequally or, at least, strategies to implement that unequal distribution are precisely what is at work in war and in the differential treatment of catastrophes such as famine and earthquakes. When populations become implicitly framed as targets for destruction within ordinary discourse, then the frame solicits our complicity with this practice of the visual and discursive normalization of war.

But another form of solicitation is also at work in such a frame, one that would lead us to an understanding of the equal value of life from an apprehension of shared precariousness. Can we discern the way the frame normalizes destruction, and can we be solicited both ethically and politically by the lives whose precarious conditions are suspended or shut out by the frame, or whose traces the frame cannot quite efface? Our visual apprehension of war is an occasion in which we implicitly consent or dissent to war or where our ambivalent relation is formulated, where we also are able to pose questions about what and how war is presented, and what absence structures and limns this visual field. If the visual field ratifies the target as a way to conceptualize precarious populations, can we read the frame as participating in the production of precarity, inducing precarity? Under what conditions might we apprehend and analyze this very induction and participation? As we watch video or see an image, what kind of solicitation is at work? Are we being invited to take aim? Are we conscripted into the trajectory of the bullet or missile? Or is there another solicitation that works through the prior one, a solicitation to apprehend the precarious conditions of life as imposing an ethical obligation on us? Is this not precisely a solicitation to refuse the target as frame, to expose its ruse, and to insist on an ethical connection to the populations being "depicted" in this way? Does the visual also become the field in which we are solicited to assume responsibility to resist unjust war and to affirm convergent precarious conditions? But as we know, wars do not always follow such controlled plans; some populations are killed simply because they are in the way, situated in proximity to the ostensible target. That is because the destructive power of the war machine exceeds its target, invariably producing collateral damage. In the destructiveness of war, there is no way to restrict the trajectory of destruction to a single visualized aim. Invariably, the fantasy of controlled destruction undoes itself, but the frame is still there, as the controlling fantasy of the state, albeit marking its limit as well. The destructiveness that the state tries to focus on this or that population cannot be controlled, which is why there are international protocols of war that seek to protect civilian lives within war. The Goldstone Report, for instance, focuses on the destruction of civilian lives as instances of war crimes. The idea of a legal war or, indeed, a just war, relies on the controllability of instruments of destruction. But because uncontrollability is part of that very destructiveness, there is no war that fails to commit a crime against humanity, a destruction of civilian life. In other words, the international law that prohibits crimes against civilians presupposes that there can be a war without such crimes, reproduced the idea of a "clean" war whose destruction has perfect aim. Only on such a condition can we distinguish between war and crimes of war. But if there is no stable way to distinguish permissible collateral damage from the destruction of civilian life, then such crimes are inevitable, and there is no non-criminal war. In other words, wars become permissible forms of criminality, but they are never non-criminal.

In targeting populations, war seeks to manage and form populations, distinguishing those lives to be preserved from those whose lives are dispensable. War is in the business of producing and reproducing precarity, sustaining populations on the edge of death, sometimes killing its members, and sometimes not; either way, it produces precarity as the norm of everyday life. Lives under such conditions of precarity do not have to be fully eviscerated to be subject to an effective and sustained operation of violence.

My point is that such visual and conceptual frames are ways of building and destroying populations as objects of knowledge and targets of war, and that such frames are the means through which social norms are relayed and made effective. At the same time, another solicitation works through the frame, one that asks us to refuse the regulation of the senses that would accept the radical ungrievability of certain populations or, rather, the differential distribution of grievability upon which war depends. Ungrievable lives are those that cannot be lost, and cannot be destroyed, because they already inhabit a lost and destroyed zone; they are, ontologically, and from the start, already lost and destroyed, which means that when they are destroyed in war, nothing is destroyed. To destroy them actively might even seem like a kind of redundancy, or a way of simply ratifying a prior truth. So it is not just that such frames serve as a mechanism through which the living and the dead are distinguished and maintained in times of war. Rather, the time of war is precisely the time of this iteration, that is, this repeated and violent differentiation between the living and the dead.

But if certain schemes operate to distinguish from the start who counts as living and who does not, how are we to count the war dead? If all war brings with it crimes of war, the targeted and collateral destruction of populations, how do such populations count when the rationale for the destruction is that they do not count at all? The reporting of the number of war dead, including civilian losses, can be one of the operations of war waging, a discursive means through which war is built,

and one way in which we are conscripted into the war
effort. Numbers, especially the number of war dead,
circulate not only as representations of war, but as part
of the apparatus of war waging. Numbers are a way to
frame the losses of war, but this does not mean that we
know whether, when, or how numbers count. We may
know how to count, or we may well rely on the reliability
of certain humanitarian or human rights organizations to
count well, but that is not the same as figuring out how
and whether a life counts. Although numbers cannot tell
us precisely whose lives count, and whose deaths count,
we can note how numbers are framed and unframed to
find out how norms that differentiate livable and grievable
lives are at work in the context of war.

   Invariably, when an assault breaks out, such as the Israeli
war on Gaza in December of 2008 and January of 2009
that took place under the name "Operation Cast Lead,"
we can start with the numbers, counting the injured and
the dead as a way of taking stock of the losses. We can also
tell and relay anecdotes that, along with numbers, start
to develop an understanding of what has happened. At
the same time, I am not sure that numbers or anecdotes,
though modes of taking account, can alone answer the
question of whose lives count, and whose lives do not.
Even when it proves possible to know what the numbers
are, the numbers may not matter at all. In other words,
there are situations when counting clearly does not count.
Some people are horrified to learn the number of war dead,
but for others, those numbers do not matter. Under what
conditions, then, do numbers count, for whom, and why?
And why is it that sometimes numbers do not count at all?

   Of course, there is something paradoxical here, since
we are used to hearing, for instance, that quantitative
methods reign in the social sciences, and that qualitative
approaches do not "count" for very much at all. And
yet, in other domains of life, numbers are remarkably
powerless. This suggests that certain implicit schemes of

conceptualization operate quite powerfully to orchestrate what we can admit as reality; they function through ritualized forms of disavowal, so even the positivist weight of numbers does not stand a chance against them. Indeed, we might imagine that if someone, anyone, were to know how many women and children have died in Gaza that they would feel outrage. That category, "women and children" has a certain salience, makes a certain emotional claim, since both categories designate presumptively innocent populations. We may imagine that no frame or matrix is needed through which to know such facts, and that knowing them would lead immediately to outrage. Or we may think that the popular disposition to object to the killing of women and children is so strong that any effort to dismiss the seriousness of these war crimes would be easily defeated. And yet, we can see how the matrix through which grievability is made possible is operative in the case of Gaza. On the one hand, it is always possible to argue: we do not know exactly whether all minors— under eighteen—are in the category of the child. But let us presume for the moment that there is something like a general disposition, broadly cultivated and operative in a wide range of cultural contexts, to regard the death of women and children as unjust and unacceptable forms of civilian casualties in war. I want to suggest that it may be possible to have this point of view, but to question whether the women and children ought really to be conceived as women and children, whether they operate in the same way that women and children do, or whether, in fact, they ought to be named and regarded in a fully different way. Once that happens, one can hold to the general view that the killing of women and children is an unacceptable part of war, but maintain, through a complicated form of disavowal and rationalization, that these deaths do not fall under that category. I want to suggest that this form of reasoning was quite popular in the Israeli press in the aftermath of that assault on Gaza. The numbers were known, but they did not count. And that is because the assaulted and destroyed body was already conceived as a pure instrument of war.

Numbers do not speak for themselves. I hope to offer a way of counting the war dead that is *not* part of the framing of the war—indeed, I am trying to offer something other than an act of war. My interest here is guided by a normative principle that the radical inequality that characterizes the difference between grievable and ungrievable lives is something that we all must struggle to overcome in the name of an interdependent world and within the terms of a more radical and effective form of egalitarianism. So, I offer the numbers here with the aim of trying to ameliorate that inequality, one that pervades dominant schemes of conceptualization and affect. So yes, there is a normative framework within which these numbers appear, but I want to suggest that it is one that opposes war, and is not part of the war effort.

The Palestinian Center for Human Rights sought to count the casualties of the twenty-two-day assault on Gaza. The last documented number I found was that 1,417 Palestinians were killed and 4,336 wounded, and that the vast majority in both categories were civilians. The United Nations special rapporteur, Richard Falk, offered slightly different numbers: 1,434 Palestinians killed in the Gaza invasion, of whom 960 were civilians, and among those civilians, there were 121 women and 288 children, although other statistics claim 313 children and youth. Israel has sought to dispute all of these numbers, accusing Hamas of inflating the number of civilian casualties, saying it can name more than 700 Hamas militants killed in the fighting. Even if we grant that point, that leaves between 500 and nearly 1,000 Palestinian civilians dead. It seems clear that the number we settle upon depends upon how we understand the category of "civilian." And to understand how that category works, we have to ask whether anyone who is understood to belong to Hamas can still be considered a civilian, and then, secondly, whether it is finally knowable within Gaza, or from an aerial view, whether someone is or is not Hamas. Let us remember that Hamas itself has its civilian and military wings, so when we say that the war dead were "Hamas," we have not said which part of Hamas, and perhaps that makes a difference. If we understand Hamas to have organized and sustained civil society in Gaza, then Hamas is not fully dissociable from civilian life. That would mean that it might not be possible to distinguish between who is Hamas and who is civilian. Indeed, one reason that Israel has refused to admit humanitarian aid into Gaza is that it does not want the already established food distribution systems, run by Hamas, to be ratified or legitimated by the distribution efforts. This means that Israel—by which I mean the government—acknowledges that Hamas is coextensive with civil society and with the material infrastructure of Gaza. If we understand that only some part of Hamas is engaged in fighting (and that in some instances it is splinter groups, themselves opposed to Hamas), and other parts of Hamas are part of a civil police force, and yet others are working on irrigation, water, food, transportation, and shelter, then what do we mean when we say that some of those killed were part of "Hamas"?

And here are some further numbers, also undisputed: Over 80 percent of the population of 1.5 million (compared to 63 percent in 2006) is dependent on international food assistance, which was dramatically reduced, and brought to a full standstill under the recent siege. The issue of starvation in Gaza has been discussed for some time. Over a year before this most recent assault, 87 percent of Gazans already lived below the poverty line, a number that had tripled since 2000. After the recent assault, it is predicted that close to 95 percent of the population will be living below the poverty line. In a November 2007 report, the Red Cross stated regarding the food allowed into Gaza that people are getting "enough to survive,

[but] not enough to live." B'tselem reports that 20,000 Gazans remain homeless after the destruction of their residences. And in the last year, we know through a series of documented anecdotes about those who lost their lives without adequate food, especially those with serious and untreated medical conditions.

It is always possible to listen to such numbers and to set them aside, or to listen to the numbers, but hear something other than the numbers, or to listen to the numbers and let them function as numbers with no referential force. Similarly, some may presume that anyone who offers such numbers has taken sides, is anti-Israel, or is not interested in the "whole story" or "the full picture." But let us remember that Jewish groups are quite active in the critique of the Israeli state and its occupation, and that even those who care about the future of Israel have argued that its militarism is self-destructive. If one sets aside the numbers because one fears the political conclusion that they support, then one blinds oneself to the numbers in order to ward off any challenge to one's already established political point of view. Of course, it is still possible to read or hear such statistics, and to not deny them, but to insist that they do not finally matter—it may be a matter of indifference, or it may be that such suffering is understood as deserved, or it may be something else: a form of righteous coldness cultivated over time through local and collective practices of nation-building, supported by prevalent social norms as they are articulated by both public policy, dominant media, and the strategies of war. These are ways of countering or quelling modes of indignation that might translate into calls for the end to violence. Righteous coldness is not only what it takes to kill, but also what is required to look on the destruction of life with moral satisfaction, even moral triumph.

We might then analyze some of the cultural tributaries of military power in Israel during the assault on Gaza— and the ongoing siege—as attempting to maximize precariousness for others while minimizing precariousness for Israel. This is, of course, a strategy that seeks to manage the unmanageable and that cannot work precisely because it disowns a common exposure to violence, by establishing the territory of Gaza as an open-air prison, as radically, if not permanently, unprotected and exposed to destruction at the same time that Israel phantasmically walls itself off from that possibility. The generalized condition or precariousness that establishes a certain equality of exposure is denied in favor of a differential distribution of precarity. Of course, this cannot work since to heighten precariousness for the other at the expense of one's own will lead to certain kinds of consequences, namely, the other will seek to invoke those same principles of self-defense that are monopolized in this instance by the colonizing power. And whereas the self-defense of the colonizer is given infinite capacity to justify acts of violent destruction, any efforts on the part of the colonized to defend life and land are taken as evidence of "inherent" violence or pre-modern tribalism. Even though this is a fairly predictable result, my argument is not finally a consequentialist one. My point is that this logic is one that cannot hold, not because we are rational creatures, but because we are invariably exposed to suffering and death through political arrangements that fail to supply protections and entitlements to life and land. Precariousness is not simply an existential condition of individuals, but rather a social condition from which certain clear political demands and principles emerge. Under political conditions in which the denial of the colonizer's precariousness in the name of invulnerable self-defense seeks to deny the condition in which human animals are each exposed to the other, and where precariousness is a generalized condition of living beings. Thus precariousness does not uniquely characterize a human life, but neither is human life exempt from the exigencies that attend to all living beings.

This way of being bound to one another in precariousness is not precisely a social bond that is entered into through volition and deliberation; it precedes contract, and is often effaced by those forms of social contract that depend on an ontology of volitional individuals. It is to the stranger that we are bound, the one, or the ones, we never knew and never chose. To kill the other is to deny my life, not just mine alone, but that sense of my life which is, from the start, and invariably, social life. This generalized truth is manifest in some explicit ways in the relation between Israel (what is called "Israel"—its borders constantly expand and it is difficult to localize at any given moment) and "Palestine" (its borders contract all the time), since they are joined inextricably, without contract, without reciprocal agreement, and yet ineluctably. So the question emerges: what obligations are to be derived from this dependency, contiguity and unwilled proximity that now defines each population, which exposes each to the fear of destruction, which incites destructiveness in the absence of any durable political structures? How are we to understand such bonds without which neither population can live and survive, and to what obligations do they lead?

This undeniable situation of proximity and inter-dependency, of vulnerability, is nevertheless denied. Let us return to the category of the civilian in order to understand how this denial takes place. There are those in the Israeli press who say that if civilians were killed, if children were killed, it was because Hamas hides itself in civilian centers, uses children to shield itself, and so sets up the situation in which Israel must kill civilians and children in order to defend itself, legitimately, against Hamas. Hamas is accused of "cynically" using children and civilian centers to hide its own armaments. There are several sources that can document the untruth of these claims, but for the moment, let us consider how this argument works. If the Palestinian children who are killed by mortar and phosphorous bombs are human shields, then they are not children at all, but rather bits of armament, military instruments and materiel, aiding and abetting an assault on Israel.

The Israelis, as we know, have targeted schools, open playgrounds, and UN compounds. So in what sense could such assaults be construed as justifiable self-defense? Still the hyper-defensive claim is made that this is Hamas' fault—the use of children as human shields—and we heard the same argument against Hezbollah in Southern Lebanon. I am wondering: are all children human shields? Only some? Are we supposed to understand Palestinian children as nothing but so many shields? If this Israeli view is right, then the children who have been killed by Israeli military aggression were already transformed into military instruments, shields that let attackers attack. If one "feels" for the children or, indeed, if one comes to regard the children as those whose lives are being unjustly and brutally destroyed in an instant, and in grotesque and appalling ways, then that kind of "sentiment" has to be over-ridden by a righteous and cold military rationality. Indeed, it is not only a cold military rationality, but one that prides itself on its ability to see and feel past the vision of massive human suffering in the name of an infinitely expanding rationale of self-defense. We are asked to believe that those children are not really children, are not really alive, that they have *already* been turned to metal, to steel, that they belong to the machinery of bombardment, at which point the body of the child is conceived as nothing more than a militarized metal that protects the attacker against attack. The only way to defend oneself against this attack is, then, to kill this child, all the children, the whole cluster; and if the United Nations defends their rights, then the UN facility should really be destroyed as well. If one were to conceptualize the child as something other than part of the defensive and manipulative machinery of war, then there would be some chance of understanding this life as a life worth living, worth sheltering, and worth grieving. But once transformed into duplicitous shrapnel, even the Palestinian child is no longer living, but is, rather, regarded as a threat to life. Indeed, there is no life other than Israeli life that counts as life to be defended at all costs. And though we can count the number of Palestinian civilians and children dead, we cannot count them. We have to continue to count them again and again. We have to start to count them, as if we have never yet learned how to count. How and when does a population begin to count? What radical changes in matrix and frame allow for the breaking out of those numbers as the animated traces of so many lives? And under what condition do those numbers efface the trace of the living, and so fail to count? Under what conditions does grievability become possible?

But, someone might object, what about the Israelis in the villages in the south of Israel? Do those lives not count? They surely do, and I say this, not only noting that they have counted, they have been acknowledged, but also that they ought to be counted. Amnesty USA reports that "Palestinian rocket attacks killed three Israeli civilians and caused severe injuries to 4 people, moderate injuries to 11, and light injuries to 167 others … (that) six Israeli soldiers were killed in the attacks by Palestinian armed groups (and 4 other were killed by Israeli forces in 'friendly fire' incidents), [and that] several hundred rockets in all were fired by Palestinian armed groups on Southern Israel."[3]

Although the numbers show us that the Palestinian losses are enormous in comparison with the Israeli ones, it does not suffice to simply make a comparison of that kind. The point is not to achieve an equality of losses. One would not want to argue that there ought to be as much destruction on the Israeli side. The point is to oppose the destruction in all of its forms in the name of a livable mode of co-habitation.

Even if there are significantly fewer Israelis who have died from this conflict than Palestinians, it remains true not only for Israelis but for most every public media, that the graphics of Israeli life, death, and detention are

---

3   http://www.amnestyusa.org/document.php?id=ENGMDE150212009

more vibrant; it conforms to the norm of human life already established, is then more of a life, is life, whereas Palestinian life is either no life, a shadow-life, or a threat to life as we know it. In this last form, it has undergone a full transformation into arsenal or spectral threat, figuring an infinite threat against which a limitless "defense" formulates itself. That defense without limit then embodies the principles of attack without limit (without shame, and without regard for established international protocols regarding war crimes).[4]

We may concur that we oppose the slaughter of innocent civilians in principle, and even if we oppose it no matter where it happens, and we oppose it no matter who does it, and which people suffer it. But this principle is only effectively applied if "slaughter" is what we are willing to call the destruction of children playing in their schoolyards, and only if we are able to apprehend as "living" those targeted populations. In other words, if certain populations—and the Palestinians are clearly prominent among them—do not count as living beings, if their very bodies are construed as instruments of war or pure vessels of attack, then they are already deprived of life before they are killed, transformed into inert matter or destructive instrumentalities, and so buried before they have had a chance to live, or to become worthy of destruction, paradoxically, in the name of life. To kill such a person, indeed, such a population, thus calls upon a racism that differentiates in advance who will count as a

---

4 Consider these numbers published by Btselem, the Israeli human rights network, regularly referenced by the Israeli government website. In the three years after the withdrawal from Gaza in 2005, 11 Israelis were killed by rocket fire—the Qassam rockets launched from the north of Gaza into Israel. On the other hand, in 2005–7 alone, the Israeli military forces killed 1,290 Palestinians in Gaza, including 222 children—and this is prior to the most recent war. Of course, one is struck by the massive disproportion, but consider as well that the numbers—and their distribution over the prior months—suggest that it is wrong to think that Hamas cannot or will not lay down its arms under any conditions.

life, and who will not. So by the time we seek to apply the norm, "thou shalt not kill," we have already lost sight of what and who is alive. Under such conditions, it becomes possible to think that ending life in the name of defending life is possible, even righteous. We fail to grasp that "life" is redoubled in such a formulation, that the one life cannot be fully dissociated from the other. And it is not as "humans" that we are bound together, but human animals whose survival depends on the workable political organization of social conditions of both unwilled proximity and interdependency. Of course, it is possible, even actual, to try to allocate death to others and reserve life for oneself, but that is to fail to understand that the life of the one is bound to the life of the other, and that certain obligations emerge from this most basic social condition. Sometimes we are able to apprehend that we are bound to each other in this way, and that precarity is one basis for claiming the equal value of lives. Such apprehension takes place at the limits of established norms of recognition, especially when those norms are in the service of war waging. Such an apprehension lets us know that precarity haunts every norm of recognition in the context of war. Such norms are articulated through media frames, through discourse, number, and image that circulate in ways that are neither static nor predictable. When the frames of war break up or break open, when the trace of lives is apprehended at the margin of what appears or as riddling its surface, then frames unwittingly establish a grievable population despite a prevalent interdiction, and there emerges the possibility of a critical outrage, war stands the chance of missing its mark.

May 2010
Berkeley, California

INTRODUCTION

Precarious Life, Grievable Life

This book consists of five essays written in response to contemporary war, focusing on cultural modes of regulating affective and ethical dispositions through a selective and differential framing of violence. In some ways the book follows on from *Precarious Life*, published by Verso in 2004, especially its suggestion that specific lives cannot be apprehended as injured or lost if they are not first apprehended as living. If certain lives do not qualify as lives or are, from the start, not conceivable as lives within certain epistemological frames, then these lives are never lived nor lost in the full sense.

On the one hand, I am seeking to draw attention to the epistemological problem raised by this issue of framing: the frames through which we apprehend or, indeed, fail to apprehend the lives of others as lost or injured (lose-able or injurable) are politically saturated. They are themselves operations of power. They do not unilaterally decide the conditions of appearance but their aim is nevertheless to delimit the sphere of appearance itself. On the other hand, the problem is ontological, since the question at issue is: *What is a life?* The "being" of life is itself constituted through selective means; as a result, we cannot refer to this "being" outside of the operations of power, and we must make more precise the specific mechanisms of power through which life is produced.

Obviously, this insight has consequences for thinking about "life" in cellular biology and the neurosciences, since certain ways of framing life inform those scientific practices as well as debates about the beginning and end of life in discussions of reproductive freedom and euthanasia. Although what I have to say may have some implications for those debates, my focus here will be on war—on why and how it becomes easier, or more difficult, to wage.

To Apprehend a Life

The precarity of life imposes an obligation upon us. We have to ask about the conditions under which it becomes possible to apprehend a life or set of lives as precarious, and those that make it less possible, or indeed impossible. Of course, it does not follow that if one apprehends a life as precarious one will resolve to protect that life or secure the conditions for its persistence and flourishing. It could be, as both Hegel and Klein point out in their different ways, that the apprehension of precariousness leads to a heightening of violence, an insight into the physical vulnerability of some set of others that incites the desire to destroy them. And yet, I want to argue that if we are to make broader social and political claims about rights of protection and entitlements to persistence and flourishing, we will first have to be supported by a new bodily ontology, one that implies the rethinking of precariousness, vulnerability, injurability, interdependency, exposure, bodily persistence, desire, work and the claims of language and social belonging.

To refer to "ontology" in this regard is not to lay claim to a description of fundamental structures of being that are distinct from any and all social and political organization. On the contrary, none of these terms exist outside of their political organization and interpretation. The "being" of the body to which this ontology refers is one that is always given over to others, to norms, to social and political organizations that have developed historically in order to maximize precariousness for some and minimize precariousness for others. It is not possible first to define the ontology of the body and then to refer to the social significations the body assumes. Rather, to be a body is to be exposed to social crafting and form, and that is what makes the ontology of the body a social ontology. In other words, the body is exposed to socially and politically articulated forces as well as to claims of sociality—including language, work, and desire—that make possible the body's persisting and flourishing. The more or less existential conception of "precariousness" is thus linked with a more specifically political notion of "precarity." And it is the differential allocation of precarity that, in my view, forms the point of departure for both a rethinking of bodily ontology and for progressive or left politics in ways that continue to exceed and traverse the categories of identity.[1]

The epistemological capacity to apprehend a life is partially dependent on that life being produced according to norms that qualify it as a life or, indeed, as part of life. In this way, the normative production of ontology thus produces the epistemological problem of apprehending a life, and this in turn gives rise to the ethical problem of what it is to acknowledge or, indeed, to guard against injury and violence. Of course, we are talking about different modalities of "violence" at each level of this analysis, but that does not mean that they are all equivalent or that no distinctions between them need to be made. The "frames" that work to differentiate the lives we can apprehend from those we cannot (or that produce lives across a continuum of life) not only organize visual experience but also generate specific ontologies of the subject. Subjects are constituted through norms which, in their reiteration, produce and shift the terms through which subjects are

---

1 For related views, see Robert Castel, *Les métamorphoses de la question sociale, une chronique du salariat*, Paris: Editions Gallimard, 1999, translated by Richard Boyd as *From Manual Workers to Wage Labourers: Transformation of the Social Question*, Edison, NJ: Transaction Publishers, 2005. See also Serge Paugam, *Le salarié de la précarité*, Paris: PUF, 2000; Nancy Ettlinger, "Precarity Unbound," *Alternatives* 32 (2007), 319–40.

recognized. These normative conditions for the production of the subject produce an historically contingent ontology, such that our very capacity to discern and name the "being" of the subject is dependent on norms that facilitate that recognition. At the same time, it would be a mistake to understand the operation of norms as deterministic. Normative schemes are interrupted by one another, they emerge and fade depending on broader operations of power, and very often come up against spectral versions of what it is they claim to know: thus, there are "subjects" who are not quite recognizable as subjects, and there are "lives" that are not quite—or, indeed, are never—recognized as lives. In what sense does life, then, always exceed the normative conditions of its recognizability? To claim that it does so is not to say that "life" has as its essence a resistance to normativity, but only that each and every construction of life requires time to do its job, and that no job it does can overcome time itself. In other words, the job is never done "once and for all." This is a limit internal to normative construction itself, a function of its iterability and heterogeneity, without which it cannot exercise its crafting power, and which limits the finality of any of its effects.

Perhaps, then, as a consequence, it is necessary to consider how we might distinguish between "apprehending" and "recognizing" a life. "Recognition" is the stronger term, one that has been derived from Hegelian texts and subject to revisions and criticisms for many years.[2] "Apprehension"

---

2   See, for example, Jessica Benjamin, *Like Subjects, Love Objects: Essays on Recognition and Sexual Difference*, New Haven: Yale University Press, 1995; Nancy Fraser, *Justice Interruptus: Critical Reflections on the "Postsocialist" Condition*, New York: Routledge, 1997; Fraser and Axel Honneth, *Redistribution or Recognition? A Political-Philosophical Exchange*, London: Verso, 2003; Axel Honneth, *The Struggle for Recognition: The Moral Grammar of Social Conflicts*, Cambridge: Polity Press, 1996; *Reification: A New Look At An Old Idea (The Berkeley Tanner Lectures)*, New York: Oxford University Press, 2008; Patchen Markell, *Bound By Recognition*, Princeton: Princeton University Press, 2003; Charles Taylor, *Hegel and Modern Society*, Cambridge: Cambridge University Press, 1979; and Taylor and Amy Gutman, eds, *Multiculturalism: Examining the Politics of Recognition*, Princeton: Princeton University Press, 1994.

is less precise, since it can imply marking, registering, acknowledging without full cognition. If it is a form of knowing, it is bound up with sensing and perceiving, but in ways that are not always—or not yet—conceptual forms of knowledge. What we are able to apprehend is surely facilitated by norms of recognition, but it would be a mistake to say that we are utterly limited by existing norms of recognition when we apprehend a life. We can apprehend, for instance, that something is not recognized by recognition. Indeed, that apprehension can become the basis for a critique of norms of recognition. The fact is we do not simply have recourse to single and discrete norms of recognition, but to more general conditions, historically articulated and enforced, of "recognizability." If we ask how recognizability is constituted, we have through the very question taken up a perspective suggesting that these fields are variably and historically constituted, no matter how *a priori* their function as conditions of appearance. If recognition characterizes an act or a practice or even a scene between subjects, then "recognizability" characterizes the more general conditions that prepare or shape a subject for recognition—the general terms, conventions, and norms "act" in their own way, crafting a living being into a recognizable subject, though not without errancy or, indeed, unanticipated results. These categories, conventions, and norms that prepare or establish a subject for recognition, that induce a subject of this kind, precede and make possible the act of recognition itself. In this sense, recognizability precedes recognition.

Frames of Recognition

How then is recognizability to be understood? In the first instance, it is *not* a quality or potential of individual humans. This may seem absurd asserted in this way, but it is important to question the idea of personhood as individualism. If we claim that recognizability is a universal potential and that it belongs to all persons as persons, then, in a way, the problem before us is already solved. We have decided that some particular notion of "personhood" will determine the scope and meaning of recognizability. Thus, we install a normative ideal as a preexisting condition of our analysis; we have, in effect, already "recognized" everything we need to know about recognition. There is no challenge that recognition poses to the form of the human that has traditionally served as the norm of recognizability, since personhood is that very norm. The point, however, will be to ask how such norms operate to produce certain subjects as "recognizable" persons and to make others decidedly more difficult to recognize. The problem is not merely how to include more people within existing norms, but to consider how existing norms allocate recognition differentially. What new norms are possible, and how are they wrought? What might be done to produce a more egalitarian set of conditions for recognizability? What might be done, in other words, to shift the very terms of recognizability in order to produce more radically democratic results?

If recognition is an act or practice undertaken by at least two subjects, and which, as the Hegelian frame would suggest, constitutes a reciprocal action, then recognizability describes those general conditions on the basis of which recognition can and does take place. It seems, then, that there are still two further terms to understand: *apprehension*, understood as a mode of knowing that is not yet recognition, or may remain irreducible to recognition; and *intelligibility*, understood as the general historical schema or schemas that establish domains of the knowable. This would constitute a dynamic field understood, at least initially, as an historical *a priori*.[3] Not all acts of knowing are acts of recognition, although the inverse claim would

---

3   For the "historical *a priori*," see Michel Foucault, *The Archaeology of Knowledge*, trans. A.M. Sheridan, London: Tavistock Publications Ltd, 1972. See also Foucault, *The Order of Things: An Archaeology of the Human Sciences*, New York: Vintage, 1970.

not hold: a life has to be intelligible *as a life*, has to conform to certain conceptions of what life is, in order to become recognizable. So just as norms of recognizability prepare the way for recognition, so schemas of intelligibility condition and produce norms of recognizability.

Those norms draw upon shifting schemes of intelligibility, so that we can and do have, for example, histories of life and histories of death. Indeed, we have ongoing debates about whether the fetus should count as life, or a life, or a human life; we have further debates about conception and what constitutes the first moments of a living organism; we have debates also about what constitutes death, whether it is the death of the brain, or of the heart, whether it is the effect of a legal declaration or a set of medical and legal certificates. All of these debates involve contested notions of personhood and, implicitly, questions regarding the "human animal" and how that conjunctive (and chiasmic) existence is to be understood. The fact that these debates exist, and continue to exist, does not imply that life and death are direct consequences of discourse (an absurd conclusion, if taken literally). Rather, it implies that there is no life and no death without a relation to some frame. Even when life and death take place between, outside, or across the frames by which they are for the most part organized, they still *take place*, though in ways that call into question the necessity of the mechanisms through which ontological fields are constituted. If a life is produced according to the norms by which life is recognized, this implies neither that everything about a life is produced according to such norms nor that we must reject the idea that there is a remainder of "life"—suspended and spectral—that limns and haunts every normative instance of life. Production is partial and is, indeed, perpetually haunted by its ontologically uncertain double. Indeed, every normative instance is shadowed by its own failure, and very often that failure assumes a figural form. The figure lays claim to no certain ontological status, and though it can be apprehended as "living," it is not always recognized as a life. In fact, a living figure outside the norms of life not only becomes the problem to be managed by normativity, but seems to be that which normativity is bound to reproduce: it is living, but not a life. It falls outside the frame furnished by the norm, but only as a relentless double whose ontology cannot be secured, but whose living status is open to apprehension.

As we know, "to be framed" is a complex phrase in English: a picture is framed, but so too is a criminal (by the police), or an innocent person (by someone nefarious, often the police), so that to be framed is to be set up, or to have evidence planted against one that ultimately "proves" one's guilt. When a picture is framed, any number of ways of commenting on or extending the picture may be at stake. But the frame tends to function, even in a minimalist form, as an editorial embellishment of the image, if not a self-commentary on the history of the frame itself.[4] This sense that the frame implicitly guides the interpretation has some resonance with the idea of the frame as a false accusation. If one is "framed," then a "frame" is constructed around one's deed such that one's guilty status becomes the viewer's inevitable conclusion. Some way of organizing and presenting a deed leads to an interpretive conclusion about the deed itself. But as we know from Trinh Minh-ha, it is possible to "frame the frame" or, indeed, the "framer,"[5] which involves exposing the ruse that produces the effect

---

4   This is, of course, more clearly the case with the caption and description, but the frame comments and editorializes in another way. My own reading of the frame here is derived from both critical and sociological sources: see especially Jacques Derrida, *The Truth of Painting*, trans. Geoff Bennington and Ian McLeod, Chicago: University of Chicago Press, 1987, 37–83. See also Erving Goffman, *Frame Analysis: An Essay on the Organization of Experience*, New York: Harper & Row, 1974; and Michel Callon, "An Essay on Framing and Overflowing: Economic Externalities Revisited by Sociology," in *The Laws of Markets*, Boston: Blackwell, 1998, 244–69.

5   Trinh T. Minh-ha, *Framer Framed*, New York: Routledge, 1992.

of individual guilt. To frame the frame seems to involve a certain highly reflexive overlay of the visual field, but, in my view, this does not have to result in rarified forms of reflexivity. On the contrary, to call the frame into question is to show that the frame never quite contained the scene it was meant to limn, that something was already outside, which made the very sense of the inside possible, recognizable. The frame never quite determined precisely what it is we see, think, recognize, and apprehend. Something exceeds the frame that troubles our sense of reality; in other words, something occurs that does not conform to our established understanding of things.

A certain leakage or contamination makes this process more fallible than it might at first appear. Benjamin's argument about the work of art in the age of mechanical reproduction can be adapted for the present moment.[6] The technical conditions of reproduction and reproducibility themselves produce a critical shifting, if not a full deterioration of context, in relation to the frames deployed by dominant media sources during times of war. This means in the first instance that even if one could, in considering global media coverage, delimit a single "context" for the creation of war photography, its circulation would necessarily depart from such a context. Although the image surely lands in new contexts, it also creates new contexts by virtue of that landing, becoming a part of the very process through which new contexts are delimited and formed. In other words, the circulation of war photos, as with the dissemination of prison poetry (in the case of the Guantánamo poets considered in Chapter 1) breaks with context all the time: in effect, the poetry leaves the prison, if it does, even when the prisoner cannot; the photos circulate on the internet, even when they were not intended for that purpose. The

---

6   Walter Benjamin, "The Work of Art in the Age of Mechanical Reproduction" (1936), in *Illuminations: Essays and Reflections*, ed. H. Arendt, trans. H. Zohn, New York: Schocken Books, 1969.

photos and poetry that fail to circulate—either because they are destroyed or because they are never permitted to leave the prison cell—are incendiary as much for what they depict as for the limitations imposed on their circulation (and very often for the way those limitations register in the images and writing themselves). This very circulability is part of what is destroyed (and if that fact then "leaks" out, the report on the destructive act circulates in the place of what is destroyed). What "gets out of hand" is precisely what breaks from the context that frames the event, the image, the text of war. But if contexts are framed (there is no context without an implicit delimitation of context), and if a frame invariably breaks from itself as it moves through space and time (if it must break from itself in order to move across space and time), then the circulating frame has to break with the context in which it is formed if it is to land or arrive somewhere else. What would it mean to understand this "breaking out" and "breaking from" as part of the media phenomena at issue, as the very function of the frame?

The frame that seeks to contain, convey, and determine what is seen (and sometimes, for a stretch, succeeds in doing precisely that) depends upon the conditions of reproducibility in order to succeed. And yet, this very reproducibility entails a constant breaking from context, a constant delimitation of new context, which means that the "frame" does not quite contain what it conveys, but breaks apart every time it seeks to give definitive organization to its content. In other words, the frame does not hold anything together in one place, but itself becomes a kind of perpetual breakage, subject to a temporal logic by which it moves from place to place. As the frame constantly breaks from its context, this self-breaking becomes part of the very definition. This leads us to a different way of understanding both the frame's efficacy and its vulnerability to reversal, to subversion, even to critical instrumentalization. What is taken for granted in one instance becomes thematized critically or even incredulously in another. This shifting temporal dimension of the frame constitutes the possibility and trajectory of its affect as well. Thus the digital image circulates outside the confines of Abu Ghraib, or the poetry in Guantánamo is recovered by constitutional lawyers who arrange for its publication throughout the world. The conditions are set for astonishment, outrage, revulsion, admiration, and discovery, depending on how the content is framed by shifting time and place. The movement of the image or the text outside of confinement is a kind of "breaking out," so that even though neither the image nor the poetry can free anyone from prison, or stop a bomb or, indeed, reverse the course of the war, they nevertheless do provide the conditions for breaking out of the quotidian acceptance of war and for a more generalized horror and outrage that will support and impel calls for justice and an end to violence.

Earlier we noted that one sense of "to be framed" means to be subject to a con, to a tactic by which evidence is orchestrated so to make a false accusation appear true. Some power manipulates the terms of appearance and one cannot break out of the frame; one is framed, which means one is accused, but also judged in advance, without valid evidence and without any obvious means of redress. But if the frame is understood as a certain "breaking out," or "breaking from," then it would seem to be more analogous to a prison break. This suggests a certain release, a loosening of the mechanism of control, and with it, a new trajectory of affect. The frame, in this sense, permits—even requires—this breaking out. This happened when the photos of Guantánamo prisoners kneeling and shackled were released to the public and outrage ensued; it happened again when the digital images from Abu Ghraib were circulated globally across the internet, facilitating a widespread visceral turn against the war. What happens at such moments? And are they merely transient moments or are they, in fact, occasions when the frame as a forcible and plausible con is exposed, resulting in a critical and exuberant release from the force of illegitimate authority?

How do we relate this discussion of frames to the problem of apprehending life in its precariousness? It may seem at first that this is a call for the production of new frames and, consequently, for new kinds of content. Do we apprehend the precariousness of life through the frames available to us, and is our task to try to install new frames that would enhance the possibility of that recognition? The production of new frames, as part of the general project of alternative media, is clearly important, but we would miss a critical dimension of this project if we restricted ourselves to this view. What happens when a frame breaks with itself is that a taken-for-granted reality is called into question, exposing the orchestrating designs of the authority who sought to control the frame. This suggests that it is not only a question of finding new content, but also of working with received renditions of reality to show how they can and do break with themselves. As a consequence, the frames that, in effect, decide which lives will be recognizable as lives and which will not, must circulate in order to establish their hegemony. This circulation brings out or, rather, *is* the iterable structure of the frame. As frames break from themselves in order to install themselves, other possibilities for apprehension emerge. When those frames that govern the relative and differential recognizability of lives come apart—as part of the very mechanism of their circulation—it becomes possible to apprehend something about what or who is living but has not been generally "recognized" as a life. What is this specter that gnaws at the norms of recognition, an intensified figure vacillating as its inside and its outside? As inside, it must be expelled to purify the norm; as outside, it threatens to undo the boundaries that limn the self. In either case, it figures the collapsibility of the norm; in other words, it is a sign that the norm functions precisely by way of managing the prospect of its undoing, an undoing that inheres in its doings.

Precariousness and Grievability

We read about lives lost and are often given the numbers, but these stories are repeated every day, and the repetition appears endless, irremediable. And so, we have to ask, what would it take not only to apprehend the precarious character of lives lost in war, but to have that apprehension coincide with an ethical and political opposition to the losses war entails? Among the questions that follow from this situation are: How is affect produced by this structure of the frame? And what is the relation of affect to ethical and political judgment and practice?

To say that a life is precarious requires not only that a life be apprehended as a life, but also that precariousness be an aspect of what is apprehended in what is living. Normatively construed, I am arguing that there ought to be a more inclusive and egalitarian way of recognizing precariousness, and that this should take form as concrete social policy regarding such issues as shelter, work, food, medical care, and legal status. And yet, I am also insisting, in a way that might seem initially paradoxical, that precariousness itself cannot be properly *recognized*. It can be apprehended, taken in, encountered, and it can be presupposed by certain norms of recognition just as it can be refused by such norms. Indeed, there ought to be recognition of precariousness as a shared condition of human life (indeed, as a condition that links human and non-human animals), but we ought not to think that the recognition of precariousness masters or captures or even fully cognizes what it recognizes. So although I would (and will) argue that norms of recognition ought to be based on an apprehension of precariousness, I do not think that precariousness is a function or effect of recognition, nor that recognition is the only or the best way to register precariousness.

To say that a life is injurable, for instance, or that it can be lost, destroyed, or systematically neglected to the point of death, is to underscore not only the finitude of a life (that death is certain) but also its precariousness (that life requires various social and economic conditions to be met in order to be sustained as a life). Precariousness implies living socially, that is, the fact that one's life is always in some sense in the hands of the other. It implies exposure both to those we know and to those we do not know; a dependency on people we know, or barely know, or know not at all. Reciprocally, it implies being impinged upon by the exposure and dependency of others, most of whom remain anonymous. These are not necessarily relations of love or even of care, but constitute obligations toward others, most of whom we cannot name and do not know, and who may or may not bear traits of familiarity to an established sense of who "we" are. In the interest of speaking in common parlance, we could say that "we" have such obligations to "others" and presume that we know who "we" are in such an instance. The social implication of this view, however, is precisely that the "we" does not, and cannot, recognize itself, that it is riven from the start, interrupted by alterity, as Levinas has said, and the obligations "we" have are precisely those that disrupt any established notion of the "we."

Over and against an existential concept of finitude that singularizes our relation to death and to life, precariousness underscores our radical substitutability and anonymity in relation both to certain socially facilitated modes of dying and death and to other socially conditioned modes of persisting and flourishing. It is not that we are born and then later become precarious, but rather that precariousness is coextensive with birth itself (birth is, by definition, precarious), which means that it matters whether or not this infant being survives, and that its survival is dependent on what we might call a social network of hands. Precisely because a living being may die, it is necessary to care for that being so that it may live. Only under conditions in which the loss would matter does the value of the life appear. Thus, grievability is a presupposition for the life that matters. For the most part, we imagine that an infant comes into the world, is sustained in and by that world through to adulthood and old age, and finally dies. We imagine that when the child is wanted, there is celebration at the beginning of life. But there can be no celebration without an implicit understanding that the life is grievable, that it would be grieved if it were lost, and that this future anterior is installed as the condition of its life. In ordinary language, grief attends the life that has already been lived, and presupposes that life as having ended. But, according to the future anterior (which is also part of ordinary language), grievability is a condition of a life's emergence and sustenance.[7] The future anterior, "a life has been lived," is presupposed at the beginning of a life that has only begun to be lived. In other words, "this will be a life that will have been lived" is the presupposition of a grievable life, which means that this will be a life that can be regarded as a life, and be sustained by that regard. Without grievability, there is no life, or, rather, there is something living that is other than life. Instead, "there is a life that will never have been lived," sustained by no regard, no testimony, and ungrieved when lost. The apprehension of grievability precedes and makes possible the apprehension of precarious life. Grievability precedes and makes possible the apprehension of the living being as living, exposed to non-life from the start.

Toward a Critique of the Right to Life

Of course, it is difficult for those on the Left to think about a discourse of "life," since we are used to thinking of those who favor increased reproductive freedoms as "pro-choice" and those who oppose them as "pro-life." But perhaps there

---

7   See Roland Barthes, *Camera Lucida: Reflections on Photography*, trans. Richard Howard, New York: Hill and Wang, 1982; and Jacques Derrida, *The Work of Mourning*, Pascale-Anne Brault and Michael Naas, eds., Chicago: University of Chicago Press, 2001.

is a way to retrieve thinking about "life" for the Left, and to make use of this framework of precarious life to sustain a strong feminist position on reproductive freedoms. One could easily see how those who take so-called "pro-life" positions might seize upon such a view to argue that the fetus is precisely this life that remains ungrieved and should be grievable, or that it is a life that is not recognized as life according to those who favor the right to abortion. Indeed, this argument could be closely linked to animal-rights claims, since one might well argue that the animal is a life that is generally not regarded as a life according to anthropocentric norms. Such debates very often turn on ontological questions, querying whether there is a significant difference between the living status of the fetus, or indeed the embryo, and that of the "person," or whether there is an ontological difference between the animal and the "human."

Let us acknowledge that these are all organisms that are living in one sense or another; to say this, however, is not yet to furnish any substantial arguments for one policy or another. After all, plants are living things, but vegetarians do not usually object to eating them. More generally, it can be argued that processes of life themselves require destruction and degeneration, but this does not in any way tell us which sorts of destruction are ethically salient and which are not. To determine the ontological specificity of life in such instances would lead us more generally into a discussion of biopolitics, concerning ways of apprehending, controlling, and administering life, and how these modes of power enter into the very definition of life itself. We would have to consider shifting paradigms within the life sciences—the shift, for example, from clinical to molecular modes of seeing, or the debates between those who prioritize cells and those who insist that tissue is the more primary unit of the living. These debates would have to be linked with new trends in biomedicalization and new modes for administering life, as well as new perspectives in biology that link the *bios* of the human with that of the animal (or that take seriously the chiasmic relation implied by the phrase, "the human animal"). We would then have to situate our discussion of war within these latter fields, which would show us how "life" itself is being defined and regenerated, as it were, within new modes of knowledge/power. I am sure it is possible to follow this path to understand the biopolitics of both war and reproductive freedom, and such paths of inquiry would be necessary to situate the discourse of life within the sphere of biopolitics and of biomedicalization more specifically. There is also, as Donna Jones has recently shown, an important link between the discourse on life, the tradition of vitalism, and various doctrines of racialism. The bibliography on these important topics has grown enormously in recent years.[8] My own contribution,

---

8   Donna Jones, *The Promise of European Decline: Vitalism, Aesthetic Politics and Race in the Inter-War Years*, Columbia University Press, forthcoming. See also: Angela Davis, *Abolition Democracy: Beyond Empire, Prisons, and Torture*, New York: Seven Stories Press, 2005; Michel Foucault, *Discipline and Punish: The Birth of the Prison*, trans. Alan Sheridan, New York: Pantheon, 1978; *Power/Knowledge: Selected Interviews and Other Writings 1972–1977*, New York: Pantheon, 1980; *Society Must Be Defended: Lectures at the College de France 1975–1976*, New York: Picador, 2003; *The Birth of Biopolitics: Lectures at the College de France 1978–1979*, New York: Palgrave Macmillan, 2008; Sarah Franklin, Celia Lury, and Jackie Stacey, *Global Nature, Global Culture*, London: Sage, 2000; Mariam Fraser, Sarah Kember, and Celia Lury, "Inventive Life: Approaches to the New Vitalism," *Theory, Culture & Society* 22: 1 (2005), 1–14; Hannah Landecker, "Cellular Features," *Critical Inquiry* 31 (2005), 903–37; Donna Haraway, *The Companion Species Manifesto: Dogs, People, and Significant Otherness*, Chicago: Prickly Paradigm Press, 2003, *Modest_Witness@Second_Millennium. FemaleMan© _Meets_ Oncomouse™*, New York: Routledge, 1997; Nicholas Rose, *The Politics of Life Itself: Biomedicine, Power, and Subjectivity in the Twenty-First Century*, Princeton: Princeton University Press, 2007; Rose and Peter Miller, *Governing the Present: Administering Economic, Social and Personal Life*, Cambridge: Polity, 2008; Paul Rabinow, *Making PCR: A Story of Biotechnology*, Chicago: University of Chicago Press, 1996; *French DNA: Trouble in Purgatory*, Chicago: University of Chicago Press, 2002; Charis Thompson, *Making Parents: The Ontological Choreography of Reproductive Technology*, Cambridge, MA: MIT Press, 2005; *Stem Cell Nations: Innovation, Ethics, and Difference in a Globalizing World*, forthcoming.

however, is not to the genealogy of the concepts of life or death, but to thinking about precariousness as something both presupposed and managed by such discourse, while never being fully resolved by any discourse.

In my view, it is not possible to base arguments for reproductive freedom, which include rights to abortion, on a conception of what is living and what is not. Stem cells are living cells, even precarious, but that does not immediately imply what policy decision ought to be made regarding the conditions under which they should be destroyed or in which they can be used. Not everything included under the rubric of "precarious life" is thus, *a priori*, worthy of protection from destruction. But these arguments become difficult precisely here, since if some living tissues or cells are worthy of protection from destruction, and others not, could this not lead to the conclusion that, under conditions of war, some human lives are worthy of protection while others are not? To see why this is a fallacious inference, we have to consider a few basic postulates of our analysis, and to see how a certain anthropocentrism conditions several questionable forms of argumentation.

The first postulate is that there is a vast domain of life not subject to human regulation and decision, and that to imagine otherwise is to reinstall an unacceptable anthropocentrism at the heart of the life sciences.

The second point is obvious, but worth restating: within that vast domain of organic life, degeneration and destruction are part of the very process of life, which means that not all degeneration can be stopped without stopping, as it were, the life processes themselves. Ironically, to rule out death for life is the death of life.

Hence, in reference to anything living, it is not possible to say in advance that there is *a right to life*, since no right can ward off all processes of degeneration and death; that pretension is the function of an omnipotent fantasy of anthropocentrism (one that seeks to deny the finitude of the *anthropos* as well).

In the same way, it does not ultimately make sense to claim, for instance, that we have to focus on what is distinctive about human life, since if it is the "life" of human life that concerns us, that is precisely where there is no firm way to distinguish in absolute terms the *bios* of the animal from the *bios* of the human animal. Any such distinction would be tenuous and would, once again, fail to see that, by definition, the human animal is itself an animal. This is not an assertion concerning the type or species of animal the human is, but an avowal that animality is a precondition of the human, and there is no human who is not a human animal.

Those who seek a basis for deciding, for instance whether or when abortion might be justified often have recourse to a moral conception of "personhood" to determine when a fetus might reasonably be called a person. Persons would then be understood as subjects of rights, entitled to protection against harm and destruction, whereas non-persons—or pre-persons, as it were—would not. Such efforts seek to settle the ethical and political questions by recourse to an ontology of personhood that relies on an account of biological individuation. Here the idea of the "person" is defined ontogenetically, by which I mean that the postulated internal development of a certain moral status or capacity of the individual becomes the salient measure by which personhood is gauged. The debate restricts itself not only to a moral domain, but to an ontology of individualism that fails to recognize that life, understood as precarious life, implies a social ontology which calls that form of individualism into question. There is no life without the conditions of life that variably sustain life, and those conditions are pervasively social, establishing not the discrete ontology of the person, but rather the interdependency of persons, involving reproducible and sustaining social relations, and relations to the environment and to non-human forms of life, broadly considered. This mode of social ontology (for which no absolute distinction between social and ecological exists) has concrete implications for how we re-approach the issues of reproductive freedom and anti-war politics. The question is not whether a given being is living or not, nor whether the being in question has the status of a "person"; it is, rather, whether the social conditions of persistence and flourishing are or are not possible. Only with this latter question can we avoid the anthropocentric and liberal individualist presumptions that have derailed such discussions.

Of course, these arguments do not yet directly address the question of under what conditions precarious life acquires a right to protection, and under what conditions it does not. One conventional way of putting this problem within moral philosophy is: Who decides, and on what basis is the decision made? But perhaps there is a more fundamental set of questions to pose: at which point does "decision" emerge as a relevant, appropriate or obligatory act? There is the question of the "who" who decides, and of the standards according to which a decision is made; but there is also the "decision" about the appropriate scope of decision-making itself. Decisions to extend life *for* humans or animals and decisions to curtail life are both notoriously controversial precisely because there is no consensus on when and where decision should enter the scene. To what extent, and with what effort and cost, can we extend livable life to the elderly or the terminally ill? Alongside religious arguments claiming that it is "not within human power" to make decisions, there are positions driven by cost-benefit analysis arguing that there are financial limits on our ability to extend life, much less livable life. But note that when we start to consider such scenarios, we imagine a group of people who are making decisions, and the decisions themselves are made in relation to an environment, broadly construed, that either will or will not make life livable. It is not simply a policy question concerning whether or not to support a life or to provide the conditions for a livable life, for implicit in our reflections is an assumption about the ontology of life itself. Simply put, life requires support and enabling conditions in order to be livable life.

Indeed, when decisions are made about providing life-extending machine support to patients, or extended nursing care to the elderly, they are made, at some level, by considering the quality and conditions of life. To say that life is precarious is to say that the possibility of being sustained relies fundamentally on social and political conditions, and not only on a postulated internal drive to live. Indeed, every drive has to be propped,[9] supported by what is outside itself, which is why there can be no persistence in life without at least some conditions that make a life livable. And this is as true for the "deciding individual" as it is for any other, including the individual who "decides" what to do about embryos, fetuses, stem cells, or random sperm. Indeed, the one who decides or asserts rights of protection does so in the context of social and political norms that frame the decision-making process, and in presumptive contexts in which the assertion of rights can be recognized. In other words, decisions are social practices, and the assertion of rights emerges precisely where conditions of interlocution can be presupposed or, minimally, invoked and incited when they are not yet institutionalized.

Perhaps most importantly, however, we would have to rethink the "right to life" where there is no final protection against destruction, and where affirmative and necessary social bonds compel us to secure the conditions for livable lives, and to do so on egalitarian grounds. This would imply positive obligations to provide those basic supports that seek to minimize precariousness in egalitarian ways:

---

9   See Freud's considerations of "Anlehnung" (anaclisis) in *Three Essays on the Theory of Sexuality* (1905), trans. James Strachey, Standard Edition, 7: 123–246, London: Hogarth Press, 1953; and "On Narcissism: An Introduction" (1914), trans. James Strachey, Standard Edition, 14: 67–102, London: Hogarth Press, 1957.

food, shelter, work, medical care, education, rights of
mobility and expression, protection against injury and
oppression. Precariousness grounds such positive social
obligations (paradoxically because precariousness is a
kind of "ungrounding" that constitutes a generalized
condition for the human animal) at the same time that
the aim of such obligations is to minimize precariousness
and its unequal distribution. In this light, then, we can
understand those modes of justifying stem-cell research
when it is clear that the use of living cells may increase the
possibilities for livable life. Similarly, the decision to abort
a fetus may well be grounded in the insight that the forms
of social and economic support needed to make that life
livable are lacking. In this sense, we can see that arguments
against certain forms of war depend on the assertion that
arbitrary modes of maximizing precariousness for some
and minimizing precariousness for others both violate basic
egalitarian norms and fail to recognize that precariousness
imposes certain kinds of ethical obligations on and among
the living.

One could object, of course, and say that the idea of
a "livable life" could give ground to those who want to
distinguish between lives worth living and lives worth
destroying—precisely the rationale that supports a
certain kind of war effort to distinguish between valuable
and grievable lives on the one hand, and devalued and
ungrievable lives on the other. But such a conclusion
neglects the important qualification that egalitarian
standards impose on the consideration of what is a livable
life. Precariousness has to be grasped not simply as a feature
of *this* or *that* life, but as a generalized condition whose very
generality can be denied only be denying precariousness
itself. And the injunction to think precariousness in
terms of equality emerges precisely from the irrefutable
generalizability of this condition. On this basis, one
objects to the differential allocation of precariousness
and grievability. Further, the very idea of precariousness

implies dependency on social networks and conditions, suggesting that there is no "life itself" at issue here, but always and only conditions of life, life as something that requires conditions in order to become livable life and, indeed, in order to become grievable.

Thus, the conclusion is not that everything that can die or is subject to destruction (i.e., all life processes) imposes an obligation to preserve life. But an obligation does emerge from the fact that we are, as it were, social beings from the start, dependent on what is outside ourselves, on others, on institutions, and on sustained and sustainable environments, and so are, in this sense, precarious. To sustain life as sustainable requires putting those conditions in place and militating for their renewal and strengthening. Where a life stands no chance of flourishing, there one must attend to ameliorating the negative conditions of life. Precarious life implies life as a conditioned process, and not as the internal feature of a monadic individual or any other anthropocentric conceit. Our obligations are precisely to the conditions that make life possible, not to "life itself," or rather, our obligations emerge from the insight that there can be no sustained life without those sustaining conditions, and that those conditions are both our political responsibility and the matter of our most vexed ethical decisions.

Political Formations

Although precarious life is a generalized condition, it is, paradoxically, the condition of being conditioned. In other words, we can say of all life that it is precarious, which is to say that life always emerges and is sustained within conditions of life. The earlier discussion of frames and norms sought to shed light on one dimension of those conditions. We cannot easily recognize life outside the frames in which it is given, and those frames not only structure how we come to know and identify life but constitute sustaining conditions for those very lives. Conditions have to be sustained, which means that they exist not as static entities, but as reproducible social institutions and relations. We would not have a responsibility to maintain conditions of life if those conditions did not require renewal. Similarly, frames are subject to an iterable structure—they can only circulate by virtue of their reproducibility, and that very reproducibility introduces a structural risk for the identity of the frame itself. The frame breaks with itself in order to reproduce itself, and its reproduction becomes the site where a politically consequential break is possible. Thus, the frame functions normatively, but it can, depending on the specific mode of circulation, call certain fields of normativity into question. Such frames structure modes of recognition, especially during times of war, but their limits and their contingency become subject to exposure and critical intervention as well.

Such frames are operative in imprisonment and torture, but also in the politics of immigration, according to which certain lives are perceived as lives while others, though apparently living, fail to assume perceptual form as such. Forms of racism instituted and active at the level of perception tend to produce iconic versions of populations who are eminently grievable, and others whose loss is no loss, and who remain ungrievable. The differential distribution of grievability across populations has implications for why and when we feel politically consequential affective dispositions such as horror, guilt, righteous sadism, loss, and indifference. Why, in particular, has there been within the US a righteous response to certain forms of violence inflicted at the same time that violence suffered by the US is either loudly mourned (the iconography of the dead from 9/11) or considered inassimilable (the assertion of masculine impermeability within state rhetoric)? If we take the precariousness of life as a point of departure, then there is no life without the need for shelter and food, no life without dependency on wider networks of sociality and labor, no life that transcends injurability and mortality.[10] We might then analyze some of the cultural tributaries of military power during these times as attempting to maximize precariousness for others while minimizing precariousness for the power in question. This differential distribution of precarity is at once a material and a perceptual issue, since those whose lives are not "regarded" as potentially grievable, and hence valuable, are made to bear the burden of starvation, underemployment, legal disenfranchisement, and differential exposure to violence and death.[11] It would be difficult, if not impossible, to decide whether the "regard"—or the failure of "regard"—leads to the "material reality" or whether the material reality leads to the failure of regard, since it would seem that both happen at once and that such perceptual categories are essential to the crafting of material reality (which does not mean that all materiality is reducible to perception, but only that perception carries its material effects).

Precariousness and precarity are intersecting concepts. Lives are by definition precarious: they can be expunged at will or by accident; their persistence is in no sense guaranteed. In some sense, this is a feature of all life, and there is no thinking of life that is not precarious—except, of course, in fantasy, and in military fantasies in particular. Political orders, including economic and social institutions, are designed to address those very needs without which the risk of mortality is heightened. Precarity designates that politically induced condition in which certain populations suffer from failing social and economic networks of support and become differentially exposed to injury, violence, and death. Such populations are at heightened risk of disease,

---

10   See especially the discussion of injurability throughout Jay Bernstein, *Adorno: Disenchantment and Ethics*, Cambridge and New York: Cambridge University Press, 2001. This remains, in my view, the most trenchant analysis of injurability and ethics in contemporary philosophy.

11   Achille Mbembe, "Necropolitics," trans. Libby Meintjes, *Public Culture* 15: 1 (2003), 11–40.

poverty, starvation, displacement, and of exposure to violence without protection. Precarity also characterizes that politically induced condition of maximized precariousness for populations exposed to arbitrary state violence who often have no other option than to appeal to the very state from which they need protection. In other words, they appeal to the state for protection, but the state is precisely that from which they require protection. To be protected from violence by the nation-state is to be exposed to the violence wielded by the nation-state, so to rely on the nation-state for protection *from* violence is precisely to exchange one potential violence for another. There may, indeed, be few other choices. Of course, not all violence issues from the nation-state, but it would be rare to find contemporary instances of violence that bear no relation to that political form.

This book considers the "frames" of war—the ways of selectively carving up experience as essential to the conduct of war. Such frames do not merely reflect on the material conditions of war, but are essential to the perpetually crafted *animus* of that material reality. There are several frames at issue here: the frame of the photograph, the framing of the decision to go to war, the framing of immigration issues as a "war at home," and the framing of sexual and feminist politics in the service of the war effort. I argue that even as the war is framed in certain ways to control and heighten affect in relation to the differential grievability of lives, so war has come to frame ways of thinking multiculturalism and debates on sexual freedom, issues largely considered separate from "foreign affairs." Sexually progressive conceptions of feminist rights or sexual freedoms have been mobilized not only to rationalize wars against predominantly Muslim populations, but also to argue for limits to immigration to Europe from predominantly Muslim countries. In the US, this has led to illegal detentions and imprisonment of those who "appear" to belong to suspect ethnic groups, although legal efforts to fight these measures have proven increasingly successful in recent years.[12] For instance, those who accept an "impasse" between sexual rights and immigration rights, especially in Europe, have failed to take into account how ongoing war has structured and fissured the subject of social movements. Understanding the cultural stakes of a war "against Islam" as it assumes a new form in coercive immigration politics challenges the Left to think beyond the established frameworks of multiculturalism and to contextualize its recent divisions in light of state violence, the exercise of war, and the heightening of "legal violence" at the border.

In recent years, the positions associated with sexual progressive politics have been pitted against claims for new immigrant rights and new cultural changes in the US and Europe. These formulations of contradiction and impasse seem to rely on a framework that fails to think critically about how the terms of domestic politics have been disturbed and deployed by the wider aims of war. A refocusing of contemporary politics on the illegitimate and arbitrary effects of state violence, including coercive means of enforcing and defying legality, may well reorient the Left beyond the liberal antinomies on which

---

12 See, for example: Center for Constitutional Rights, "Illegal Detentions and Guantánamo," http://ccrjustice.org/illegal-detentions-and-Guantánamo; "Illegal Detentions in Iraq by US Pose Great Challenge: Annan" (Reuters), CommonDreams.org, June 9, 2005, http://www.commondreams.org/headlines05/0609-04.htm; Amnesty International USA, "Guantánamo and Illegal U.S. Detentions," http://www.amnestyusa.org/war-on-terror/Guantánamo/page.do?id=1351079; Jerry Markon, "Memo Proves Detention Is Illegal, Attorneys Say," *Washington Post*, April 9, 2008, http://www.washingtonpost.com/wp-dyn/content/article/2008/04/08/AR2008040803080.html; Giovanni Claudio Fava, "Transportation and illegal detention of prisoners by CIA," European Parliament, February 14, 2007, http://www.europarl.europa.eu/eplive/expert/shotlist_page/20070214SHL03138/default_en.htm; Hina Shamsi, "CIA Coverups and American Injustice," *Salon.com*, December 11, 2007, http://www.salon.com/opinion/feature/2007/12/11/Guantánamo/index.html

it currently founders. A coalition of those who oppose illegitimate coercion and violence, and who oppose racisms of all kinds (non-differentially), would certainly also imply a sexual politics that adamantly refuses to be appropriated as a spurious rationale for the current wars. The frameworks through which we think the Left need to be reformulated in light of new forms of state violence— especially those that seek to suspend legal constraints in the name of sovereignty, or which fabricate quasi-legal systems in the name of national security. Very often, we do not see that the ostensibly "domestic" issues are inflected by the foreign policy issues, and that a similar "frame" grounds our orientation in both domains. Nor do we always call into question this way of framing divisions between domestic and foreign issues. If such frames were brought into critical contact with one another, what kind of politics would result? It would perhaps give us a way to militate against the mobilization of "progressive" domestic agendas (feminism, sexual freedom) for war and anti-immigration politics, even for rationales for sexual torture. It would mean thinking sexual politics together with immigration politics in new ways, and considering how populations are differentially exposed to conditions that jeopardize the possibility of persisting and flourishing.

This work seeks to reorient politics on the Left toward a consideration of precarity as an existing and promising site for coalitional exchange. For populations to become grievable does not require that we come to know the singularity of every person who is at risk or who has, indeed, already been risked. Rather, it means that policy needs to understand precariousness as a shared condition, and precarity as the politically induced condition that would deny equal exposure through the radically unequal distribution of wealth and the differential ways of exposing certain populations, racially and nationally conceptualized, to greater violence. The recognition of shared precariousness introduces strong normative commitments of equality and invites a more robust universalizing of rights that seeks to address basic human needs for food, shelter, and other conditions for persisting and flourishing. We might be tempted to call these "material needs"—and that they surely are. But once we acknowledge that the "frames" through which such needs are affirmed or denied make possible the practices of war, we have to conclude that the frames of war are part of what makes the materiality of war. Just as the "matter" of bodies cannot appear without a shaping and animating form, neither can the "matter" of war appear without a conditioning and facilitating form or frame. The operation of cameras, not only in the recording and distribution of images of torture, but as part of the very apparatus of bombing, make it clear that media representations have already become modes of military conduct.[13] So there is no way to separate, under present historical conditions, the material reality of war from those representational regimes through which it operates and which rationalize its own operation. The perceptual realities produced through such frames do not precisely lead to war policy, and neither do such policies unilaterally create frames of perception. Perception and policy are but two modalities of the same process whereby the ontological status of a targeted population is compromised and suspended. This is not the same as "bare life," since the lives in question are not cast outside the polis in a state of radical exposure, but bound and constrained by power relations in a situation of forcible exposure. It is not the withdrawal or absence of law that produces precariousness, but the very effects of illegitimate legal coercion itself, or the exercise of state power freed from the constraints of all law.

These reflections have implications for thinking through the body as well, since there are no conditions that can

---

13   See my essay "The Imperialist Subject," *Journal of Urban and Cultural Studies* 2: 1 (1991), 73–8.

fully "solve" the problem of human precariousness. Bodies come into being and cease to be: as physically persistent organisms, they are subject to incursions and to illnesses that jeopardize the possibility of persisting at all. These are necessary features of bodies—they cannot "be" thought without their finitude, and they depend on what is "outside themselves" to be sustained—features that pertain to the phenomenological structure of bodily life. To live is always to live a life that is at risk from the outset and can be put at risk or expunged quite suddenly from the outside and for reasons that are not always under one's control.

Whereas most positions derived from Spinozistic accounts of bodily persistence emphasize the body's productive desire,[14] have we yet encountered a Spinozistic account of bodily vulnerability or considered its political implications?[15] The *conatus* can be and is undercut by any number of sources: we are bound to others not only through networks of libidinal connection, but also through modes of unwilled dependency and proximity that may well entail ambivalent psychic consequences, including binds of aggression and desire (Klein).[16] Moreover, this generalized condition of precariousness and dependency is exploited and disavowed in particular political formations. No amount of will or wealth can eliminate the possibilities of illness or accident for a living body, although both can be mobilized in the service of such an illusion. These risks are built into the very conception of bodily life considered both finite and precarious, implying that the body is

---

14   Benedict de Spinoza, *A Spinoza Reader: The* Ethics *and Other Works*, ed. and trans. Edwin Curley, Princeton, NJ: Princeton University Press, 1994. See also Gilles Deleuze, *Expressionism in Philosophy: Spinoza*, trans. Martin Joughin, New York: Zone Books, 1992.

15   Deleuze clearly approaches this with his discussion of "what can a body do?" in *Expressionism in Philosophy: Spinoza*.

16   Melanie Klein, "A Contribution to the Psychogenesis of Manic-Depressive States," *Selected Melanie Klein*, ed. Juliet Mitchell, London: Penguin, 1986, 115–46.

always given over to modes of sociality and environment that limit its individual autonomy. The shared condition of precariousness implies that the body is constitutively social and interdependent—a view clearly confirmed in different ways by both Hobbes and Hegel. Yet, precisely because each body finds itself potentially threatened by others who are, by definition, precarious as well, forms of domination follow. This standard Hegelian point takes on specific meanings under contemporary conditions of war: the shared condition of precariousness leads not to reciprocal recognition, but to a specific exploitation of targeted populations, of lives that are not quite lives, cast as "destructible" and "ungrievable." Such populations are "lose-able," or can be forfeited, precisely because they are framed as being already lost or forfeited; they are cast as threats to human life as we know it rather than as living populations in need of protection from illegitimate state violence, famine, or pandemics. Consequently, when such lives are lost they are not grievable, since, in the twisted logic that rationalizes their death, the loss of such populations is deemed necessary to protect the lives of "the living."

This consideration of the differential distribution of precariousness and grievability constitutes an alternative to those models of multiculturalism that presuppose the nation-state as the exclusive frame of reference, and pluralism as an adequate way of thinking about heterogeneous social subjects. Although certain liberal principles remain crucial to this analysis, including equality and universality, it remains clear that liberal norms presupposing an ontology of discrete identity cannot yield the kinds of analytic vocabularies we need for thinking about global interdependency and the interlocking networks of power and position in contemporary life. Part of the very problem of contemporary political life is that not everyone counts as a subject. Multiculturalism tends to presuppose already constituted communities, already established subjects, when what is at stake are communities not quite recognized as such, subjects who are living, but not yet regarded as "lives." Further, the problem is not simply one of co-existence, but of how the politics of differential subject formation within contemporary maps of power seek (a) to mobilize sexual progressives against new immigrants in the name of a spurious conception of freedom, and (b) to deploy gender and sexual minorities in the rationalization of recent and current wars.

Left politics in this regard would aim first to refocus and expand the political critique of state violence, including both war and those forms of legalized violence by which populations are differentially deprived of the basic resources needed to minimize precariousness. This seems urgently necessary in the context of crumbling welfare states and those in which social safety nets have been torn asunder or denied the chance to emerge. Second, the focus would be less on identity politics, or the kinds of interests and beliefs formulated on the basis of identity claims, and more on precarity and its differential distributions, in the hope that new coalitions might be formed capable of overcoming the sorts of liberal impasses mentioned above. Precarity cuts across identity categories as well as multicultural maps, thus forming the basis for an alliance focused on opposition to state violence and its capacity to produce, exploit, and distribute precarity for the purposes of profit and territorial defense. Such an alliance would not require agreement on all questions of desire or belief or self-identification. It would be a movement sheltering certain kinds of ongoing antagonisms among its participants, valuing such persistent and animating differences as the sign and substance of a radical democratic politics.

1

Survivability, Vulnerability, Affect

The postulation of a generalized precariousness that calls into question the ontology of individualism implies, although does not directly entail, certain normative consequences. It does not suffice to say that since life is precarious, therefore it must be preserved. At stake are the conditions that render life sustainable, and thus moral disagreements invariably center on how or whether these conditions of life can be improved and precarity ameliorated. But if such a view entails a critique of individualism, how do we begin to think about ways to assume responsibility for the minimization of precarity? If the ontology of the body serves as a point of departure for such a rethinking of responsibility, it is precisely because, in its surface and its depth, the body is a social phenomenon: it is exposed to others, vulnerable by definition. Its very persistence depends upon social conditions and institutions, which means that in order to "be," in the sense of "persist," it must rely on what is outside itself. How can responsibility be thought on the basis of this socially ecstatic structure of the body? As something that, by definition, yields to social crafting and force, the body is vulnerable. It is not, however, a mere surface upon which social meanings are inscribed, but that which suffers, enjoys, and responds to the exteriority of the world, an exteriority that defines its disposition, its passivity and activity. Of course, injury is one thing that can and does happen to a vulnerable body (and there are no invulnerable bodies), but that is not to say that the body's vulnerability is reducible to its injurability. That the body invariably comes up against the outside world is a sign of the general predicament of unwilled proximity to others and to circumstances beyond one's control. This "coming up against" is one modality that defines the body. And yet, this obtrusive alterity against which the body finds itself can be, and often is, what animates responsiveness to that world. That responsiveness may include a wide range of affects: pleasure, rage, suffering, hope, to name a few.

Such affects, I would argue, become not just the basis, but the very stuff of ideation and of critique.[1] In this way, a certain interpretive act implicitly takes hold at moments of primary affective responsiveness. Interpretation does not emerge as the spontaneous act of a single mind, but as a consequence of a certain field of intelligibility that helps to form and frame our responsiveness to the impinging world (a world on which we depend, but which also impinges upon us, exacting responsiveness in complex, sometimes ambivalent, forms). Hence, precariousness as a generalized condition relies on a conception of the body as fundamentally dependent on, and conditioned by, a sustained and sustainable world; responsiveness—and thus, ultimately, responsibility—is located in the affective responses to a sustaining and impinging world. Because such affective responses are invariably mediated, they call upon and enact certain interpretive frames; they can also call into question the taken-for-granted character of those frames, and in that way provide the affective conditions for

---

1   See Lauren Berlant, ed., *Intimacy*, Chicago: University of Chicago, 2000; Ann Cvetkovich, *An Archive of Feelings: Trauma, Sexuality, and Lesbian Public Cultures*, Raleigh, NC: Duke University Press, 2003; Sara Ahmed, *The Cultural Politics of Emotion*, Edinburgh: Edinburgh University Press, 2004.

social critique. As I have argued elsewhere, moral theory has to become social critique if it is to know its object and act upon it. To understand the schema I have proposed in the context of war, it is necessary to consider how responsibility must focus not just on the value of this or that life, or on the question of survivability in the abstract, but on the sustaining social conditions of life—especially when they fail. This task becomes particularly acute in the context of war.

It is not easy to turn to the question of responsibility, not least since the term itself has been used for ends that are contrary to my purpose here. In France, for instance, where social benefits to the poor and new immigrants have been denied, the government has called for a new sense of "responsibility," by which it means that individuals ought not to rely on the state but on themselves. A word has even been coined to describe the process of producing self-reliant individuals: "responsibilization." I am certainly not opposed to individual responsibility, and there are ways in which, to be sure, we all must assume responsibility for ourselves. But a few critical questions emerge for me in light of this formulation: am I responsible only to myself? Are there others for whom I am responsible? And how do I, in general, determine the scope of my responsibility? Am I responsible for all others, or only to some, and on what basis would I draw that line?

This is, however, only the beginning of my difficulties. I confess to having some problems with the pronouns in question. Is it only as an "I," that is, as an individual, that I am responsible? Could it be that when I assume responsibility what becomes clear is that who "I" am is bound up with others in necessary ways? Am I even thinkable without that world of others? In effect, could it be that through the process of assuming responsibility the "I" shows itself to be, at least partially, a "we"?

But who then is included in the "we" that I seem to be, or to be part of? And for which "we" am I finally responsible? This is not the same as the question: to which "we" do I belong? If I identify a community of belonging on the basis of nation, territory, language, or culture, and if I then base my sense of responsibility on that community, I implicitly hold to the view that I am responsible only for those who are recognizably like me in some way. But what are the implicit frames of recognizability in play when I "recognize" someone as "like" me? What implicit political order produces and regulates "likeness" in such instances? What is our responsibility toward those we do not know, toward those who seem to test our sense of belonging or to defy available norms of likeness? Perhaps we belong to them in a different way, and our responsibility to them does not in fact rely on the apprehension of ready-made similitudes. Perhaps such a responsibility can only begin to be realized through a critical reflection on those exclusionary norms by which fields of recognizability are constituted, fields that are implicitly invoked when, by a cultural reflex, we mourn for some lives but respond with coldness to the loss of others.

Before I suggest a way of thinking about global responsibility during these times of war, I want to distance myself from some mistaken ways of approaching the problem. Those, for instance, who wage war in the name of the common good, those who kill in the name of democracy or security, those who make incursions into the sovereign lands of others in the name of sovereignty—all consider themselves to be "acting globally" and even to be executing a certain "global responsibility." In the US we have heard in recent years about "bringing democracy" to countries where it is apparently lacking; we have heard, too, about "installing democracy." In such moments we have to ask what democracy means if it is not based on popular decision and majority rule. Can one power "bring" or "install" democracy on a people over whom it has no jurisdiction? If a form of power is imposed upon a people who do not choose that form of power, then that is, by definition, an undemocratic process. If the form of power imposed is called "democracy" then we have an even larger problem: can "democracy" be the name of a form of political power that is undemocratically imposed? Democracy has to name the means through which political power is achieved as well as the result of that process. And this creates something of a bind, since a majority can certainly vote in an undemocratic form of power (as the Germans did when electing Hitler in 1933), but military powers can also seek to "install" democracy through overriding or suspending elections and other expressions of the popular will, and by means that are patently undemocratic. In both cases, democracy fails.

How do these brief reflections on the perils of democracy affect our way of thinking about global responsibility in times of war? First, we must be wary of invocations of "global responsibility" which assume that one country has a distinctive responsibility to bring democracy to other countries. I am sure that there are cases in which intervention is important—to forestall genocide, for instance. But it would be a mistake to conflate such an intervention with a global mission or, indeed, with an arrogant politics in which forms of government are forcibly implemented that are in the political and economic interests of the military power responsible for that very implementation. In such cases, we probably want to say—or at least I want to say— that this form of global responsibility is irresponsible, if not openly contradictory. We could say that in such instances the word "responsibility" is simply misused or abused. And I would tend to agree. But that may not be enough, since historical circumstances demand that we give new meanings to the notion of "responsibility." Indeed, there is a challenge before us to rethink and reformulate a conception of global responsibility that would counter this imperialist appropriation and its politics of imposition.

To that end, I want to return to the question of the "we" and think first about what happens to this "we" during

times of war. Whose lives are regarded as lives worth saving
and defending, and whose are not? Second, I want to ask
how we might rethink the "we" in global terms in ways
that counter the politics of imposition. Lastly, and in the
chapters to come, I want to consider why the opposition
to torture is obligatory, and how we might derive an
important sense of global responsibility from a politics that
opposes the use of torture in any and all of its forms.[2]

So, one way of posing the question of who "we" are in
these times of war is by asking whose lives are considered
valuable, whose lives are mourned, and whose lives are
considered ungrievable. We might think of war as dividing
populations into those who are grievable and those who
are not. An ungrievable life is one that cannot be mourned
because it has never lived, that is, it has never counted
as a life at all. We can see the division of the globe into
grievable and ungrievable lives from the perspective of
those who wage war in order to defend the lives of certain
communities, and to defend them against the lives of
others—even if it means taking those latter lives. After
the attacks of 9/11, we encountered in the media graphic
pictures of those who died, along with their names, their
stories, the reactions of their families. Public grieving was
dedicated to making these images iconic for the nation,
which meant of course that there was considerably less
public grieving for non-US nationals, and none at all for
illegal workers.

The differential distribution of public grieving is a
political issue of enormous significance. It has been since
at least the time of Antigone, when she chose openly to
mourn the death of one of her brothers even though it
went against the sovereign law to do so. Why is it that

---

2   For this purpose, see Karen J. Greenberg, ed., *The Torture Debate in America*,
New York: Cambridge University Press, 2006; Kim Scheppele, "Hypothetical
Torture in the 'War on Terrorism'," *Journal of National Security Law and Policy*
1 (2005), 285–340.

governments so often seek to regulate and control who will be publicly grievable and who will not? In the initial years of the AIDS crisis in the US, the public vigils, and the Names Project[3] broke through the public shame associated with dying from AIDS, a shame associated sometimes with homosexuality, and especially anal sex, and sometimes with drugs and promiscuity. It meant something to state and show the name, to put together some remnants of a life, to publicly display and avow the loss. What would happen if those killed in the current wars were to be grieved in just such an open way? Why is it that we are not given the names of all the war dead, including those the US has killed, of whom we will never have the image, the name, the story, never a testimonial shard of their life, something to see, to touch, to know? Although it is not possible to singularize every life destroyed in war, there are surely ways to register the populations injured and destroyed without fully assimilating to the iconic function of the image.[4]

Open grieving is bound up with outrage, and outrage in the face of injustice or indeed of unbearable loss has enormous political potential. It is, after all, one of the reasons Plato wanted to ban the poets from the Republic. He thought that if the citizens went too often to watch tragedy, they would weep over the losses they saw, and that such open and public mourning, in disrupting the order and hierarchy of the soul, would disrupt the order and hierarchy of political authority as well. Whether we are speaking about open grief or outrage, we are talking about affective responses that are highly regulated by regimes of power and sometimes subject to explicit censorship. In the contemporary wars in which the US

---

3   See Anthony Turney and Paul Margolies, *Always Remember: The Names Project AIDS Memorial Quilt*, New York: Fireside, 1996. See also, http://www. aidsquilt.org

4   David Simpson, *9/11: The Culture of Commemoration*, Chicago: University of Chicago Press, 2006.

is directly engaged, those in Iraq and Afghanistan, we can see how affect is regulated to support both the war effort and, more specifically, nationalist belonging. When the photos of Abu Ghraib were first released in the US, conservative television pundits argued that it would be un-American to show them. We were not supposed to have graphic evidence of the acts of torture US personnel had committed. We were not supposed to know that the US had violated internationally recognized human rights. It was un-American to show these photos and un-American to glean information from them as to how the war was being conducted. The conservative political commentator Bill O'Reilly thought that the photos would create a negative image of the US and that we had an obligation to defend a positive image.[5] Donald Rumsfeld said something similar, suggesting that it was anti-American to display the photos.[6] Of course, neither considered that the American public might have a right to know about the activities of its military, or that the public's right to judge the war on the basis of full evidence is part of the democratic tradition of participation and deliberation. So what was really being said? It seems to me that those who sought to limit the power of the image in this instance also sought to limit the power of affect, of outrage, knowing full well that it could and would turn public opinion against the war in Iraq, as indeed it did.

---

5   "But Abu Ghraib was interesting. I got criticized by the *New York Times* for not running the pictures. And I told the audience, I'll tell you what happened. I'm not running them because I know—you know, we go all over the world. And I know as soon as I run them, Al Jazeera's going to pick them off *The Factor*, throw them on there and whip up anti-US feeling—and more people are going to get killed. So I'm not going to do it. You want to see them, you can see them someplace else. Not here." *The O'Reilly Factor*, Fox News Channel, May 12, 2005.

6   See, for example, Greg Mitchell, "Judge Orders Release of Abu Ghraib Photos," *Editor and Publisher*, September 29, 2005, http://www.editorandpublisher.com/eandp/news/article_display.jsp?vnu_content_id=1001218842

The question, though, of whose lives are to be regarded as grievable, as worthy of protection, as belonging to subjects with rights that ought to be honored, returns us to the question of how affect is regulated and of what we mean by the regulation of affect at all. The anthropologist Talal Asad recently wrote a book about suicide bombing in which the first question he poses is: Why do we feel horror and moral repulsion in the face of suicide bombing when we do not always feel the same way in the face of state-sponsored violence?[7] He asks the question not in order to say that these forms of violence are the same, or even to say that we ought to feel the same moral outrage in relation to both. But he finds it curious, and I follow him here, that our moral responses—responses that first take form as affect—are tacitly regulated by certain kinds of interpretive frameworks. His thesis is that we feel more horror and moral revulsion in the face of lives lost under certain conditions than under certain others. If, for instance, someone kills or is killed in war, and the war is state-sponsored, and we invest the state with legitimacy, then we consider the death lamentable, sad, and unfortunate, but not radically unjust. And yet if the violence is perpetrated by insurgency groups regarded as illegitimate, then our affect invariably changes, or so Asad assumes.

Although Asad asks us to think about suicide bombing—something I won't do right now—it is also clear that he is saying something important about the politics of moral responsiveness; namely, that what we feel is in part conditioned by how we interpret the world around us; that how we interpret what we feel actually can and does alter the feeling itself. If we accept that affect is structured by interpretive schemes that we do not fully understand, can this help us understand why it is we might feel horror in the face of certain losses but indifference or even righteousness

---

7   Talal Asad, *On Suicide Bombing*, New York: Columbia University Press, 2007.

in light of others? In contemporary conditions of war and heightened nationalism, we imagine that our existence is bound up with others with whom we can find national affinity, who are recognizable to us, and who conform to certain culturally specific notions about what the culturally recognizable human is. This interpretative framework functions by tacitly differentiating between those populations on whom my life and existence depend, and those populations who represent a direct threat to my life and existence. When a population appears as a direct threat to my life, they do not appear as "lives," but as the threat to life (a living figure that figures the threat to life). Consider how this is compounded under those conditions in which Islam is seen as barbaric or pre-modern, as not yet having conformed to those norms that make the human recognizable. Those we kill are not quite human, and not quite alive, which means that we do not feel the same horror and outrage over the loss of their lives as we do over the loss of those lives that bear national or religious similarity to our own.

Asad wonders whether modes of death-dealing are apprehended differently, whether we object to the deaths caused by suicide bombing more forcefully and with greater moral outrage than we do to those deaths caused by aerial bombings. But here I am wondering whether there is not also a differential way of regarding populations, such that some are considered from the start very much alive and others more questionably alive, perhaps even socially dead (the term that Orlando Patterson developed to describe the status of the slave), or as living figures of the threat to life.[8] But if war or, rather, the current wars, rely on and perpetuate a way of dividing lives into those that are worth defending, valuing, and grieving when they are lost, and those that are not quite lives, not quite valuable,

---

8   Orlando Patterson, *Slavery and Social Death: A Comparative Study*, Cambridge, MA: Harvard University Press, 1982.

recognizable or, indeed, mournable, then the death of ungrievable lives will surely cause enormous outrage on the part of those who understand that their lives are not considered to be lives in any full and meaningful sense. So although the logic of self-defense casts such populations as "threats" to life as we know it, they are themselves living populations with whom cohabitation presupposes a certain interdependency among us. How that interdependency is avowed (or disavowed) and instituted (or not) has concrete implications for who survives, who thrives, who barely makes it, and who is eliminated or left to die. I want to insist on this interdependency precisely because when nations such as the US or Israel argue that their survival is served by war, a systematic error is committed. This is because war seeks to deny the ongoing and irrefutable ways in which we are all subject to one another, vulnerable to destruction by the other, and in need of protection through multilateral and global agreements based on the recognition of a shared precariousness. I think this is finally a Hegelian point, and one worth reiterating here. The reason I am not free to destroy another—and indeed, why nations are not finally free to destroy one another— is not only because it will lead to further destructive consequences. That is doubtless true. But what may be finally more true is that the subject that I am is bound to the subject I am not, that we each have the power to destroy and to be destroyed, and that we are bound to one another in this power and this precariousness. In this sense, we are all precarious lives.

After 9/11 we saw the development of the perspective according to which the "permeability of the border" represents a national threat, or indeed a threat to identity itself. Identity, however, is not thinkable without the permeable border, or else without the possibility of relinquishing a boundary. In the first case, one fears invasion, encroachment, and impingement, and makes a territorial claim in the name of self-defense. But in the other case, a boundary is given up or overcome precisely in order to establish a certain connection beyond the claims of territory. The fear of survivability can attend either gesture, and if this is so, what does it tell us about how our sense of survivability is inevitably bound up with those we do not know, who may well not be fully recognizable according to our own national or parochial norms?

According to Melanie Klein, we develop moral responses in reaction to questions of survivability.[9] My wager is that Klein is right about that, even as she thwarts her own insight by insisting that it is the ego's survivability that is finally at issue. Why the ego? After all, if my survivability depends on a relation to others, to a "you" or a set of "yous" without whom I cannot exist, then my existence is not mine alone, but is to be found outside myself, in this set of relations that precede and exceed the boundaries of who I am. If I have a boundary at all, or if a boundary can be said to belong to me, it is only because I have become separated from others, and it is only on condition of this separation that I can relate to them at all. So the boundary is a function of the relation, a brokering of difference, a negotiation in which I am bound to you in my separateness. If I seek to preserve your life, it is not only because I seek to preserve my own, but because who "I" am is nothing without your life, and life itself has to be rethought as this complex, passionate, antagonistic, and necessary set of relations to others. I may lose this "you" and any number of particular others, and I may well survive those losses. But that can happen only if I do not lose the possibility of any "you" at all. If I survive, it is only because my life is nothing without the life that exceeds me, that refers to some indexical you, without whom I cannot be.

My use of Klein here is decidedly un-Kleinian. Indeed, I believe she furnishes an analysis that compels us to move in a direction that Klein would and could never go. Let

9   Klein, "A Contribution to the Psychogenesis of Manic-Depressive States."

me consider for a moment what I think is right about Klein's insight, even as I have to disagree with Klein in her account of drives and of self-preservation and seek to develop a social ontology on the basis of her analysis— something she would have surely refused.

If guilt is linked to fears about survivability, then this suggests that, as a moral response, guilt references a pre-moral set of fears and impulses tied up with destructiveness and its consequences. If guilt poses a question for the human subject, it is not first and foremost a question of whether one is leading the good life, but of whether life will be livable at all. Whether conceived of as emotion or feeling, guilt tells us something about how the process of moralization occurs and how it deflects from the crisis of survivability itself. If one feels guilt at the prospect of destroying the object/the other to whom one is bound, the object of love and attachment, then it may be for reasons of self-preservation. If I destroy the other, then I destroy the one on whom I depend in order to survive, and so I threaten my own survival with my destructive act. If Klein is right, then, I probably don't care very much about the other person as such; they do not come into focus for me as another, separate from me, who "deserves" to live and whose life depends on my ability to check my own destructiveness. For Klein, the question of survival precedes the question of morality; indeed, it would seem that guilt does not index a moral relation to the other, but an unbridled desire for self-preservation. In Klein's view, I only want the other to survive so that I may survive. The other is instrumental to my own survival, and guilt, even morality, are simply the instrumental consequences of this desire for self-preservation, one that is threatened mainly by my own destructiveness.

Guilt would seem then to characterize a particular human capacity to assume responsibility for certain actions. I am guilty because I sought to destroy a bond that I require in order to live. Guilt appears to be a primarily self-preservative impulse, one that may well be bound up with the ego, even though, as we know, Klein herself is no ego psychologist. One might read this drive for self-preservation as a desire to preserve oneself as a human; but because it is my survival that is threatened by my destructive potential, it seems that guilt refers less to any humanness than to life, and, indeed, to survivability. Thus, only as an animal who can live or die do any of us feel guilt; only for one whose life is bound up with other lives and who must negotiate the power to injure, to kill, and to sustain life, does guilt become an issue. Paradoxically, guilt—which is so often seen as a paradigmatically human emotion, generally understood to engage self-reflective powers and so to separate human from animal life—is driven less by rational reflection than by the fear of death and the will to live. Guilt thus disputes the anthropocentrism that so often underwrites accounts of the moral sentiments and instead establishes the *anthropos* as an animal seeking survival, but one whose survivability is a function of a frail and brokered sociality. Life is sustained not by a self-preserving drive, conceived as an internal impulse of the organism, but by a condition of dependency without which survival proves impossible, but which can also imperil survival depending on the form that dependency takes.

If we take Klein's point that destructiveness is the problem for the human subject, it would seem that it is also what links the human and non-human. This seems most acutely true in times of war when sentient life of all kinds is put at heightened risk, and it seems to me acutely true for those who have the power to wage war, that is, to become subjects whose destructiveness threatens whole populations and environments. So if I conduct a certain first-world criticism of the destructive impulse in this chapter, it will be precisely because I am a citizen of a country that systematically idealizes its own capacity for murder. I think it was in the film *Rush Hour 3* that, when the lead characters get into a taxi in Paris, the taxi driver realizes they are Americans and expresses his enthusiastic interest in the impending American adventure.[10] Along the way, he offers a keen ethnographic insight: "Americans!" he says, "They kill people for no reason!" Now, of course, the US government gives all kinds of reasons for its killings while at the same time refusing to call those killings "killings" at all. But if I undertake an inquiry into this question of destructiveness, and if I turn toward the question of precariousness and vulnerability, then it is precisely because I think a certain dislocation of perspective is necessary for the rethinking of global politics. The notion of the subject produced by the recent wars conducted by the US, including its torture operations, is one in which the US subject seeks to produce itself as impermeable, to define itself as protected permanently against incursion and as radically invulnerable to attack. Nationalism works in part by producing and sustaining a certain version of the subject. We can call it imaginary, if we wish, but we have to remember that it is produced and sustained through powerful forms of media, and that what gives power to their version of the subject is precisely the way in which they are able to render the subject's own destructiveness *righteous* and its own destructibility *unthinkable*.

The question of how those relations or interdependencies are conceived is thus linked with whether and how we can extend our sense of political dependency and obligation to a global arena beyond the nation. Nationalism in the US has, of course, been heightened since the attacks of 9/11, but let us remember that this is a country that extends its jurisdiction beyond its own borders, that suspends its constitutional obligations within those borders, and that understands itself as exempt from any number of international agreements. It jealously guards its right to sovereign self-protection while making righteous incursions into other sovereignties or, in the case of

---

10   *Rush Hour 3*, dir. Brett Ratner, 2007.

Palestine, refusing to honor any principles of sovereignty at all. I want to emphasize that the move to affirm dependency and obligation outside the nation-state has to be distinguished from those forms of imperialism that assert claims of sovereignty outside the boundaries of the nation-state. This is not an easy distinction to make or to secure, but I think it presents an urgent and contemporary challenge for our times.

When I refer to a schism that structures (and de-structures) the national subject, I am referring to those modes of defense and displacement—to borrow a psychoanalytic category—that lead us, in the name of sovereignty, to defend a border in one instance and to violate it in another with impunity. The call to interdependency is also, then, a call to overcome this schism and to move toward the recognition of a generalized condition of precariousness. It cannot be that the other is destructible while I am not; nor vice versa. It can only be that life, conceived as precarious life, is a generalized condition, and that under certain political conditions it becomes radically exacerbated or radically disavowed. This is a schism in which the subject asserts its own righteous destructiveness at the same time as it seeks to immunize itself against the thought of its own precariousness. It belongs to a politics driven by horror at the thought of the nation's destructibility, or that of its allies. It constitutes a kind of unreasoned rift at the core of the subject of nationalism. The point is not to oppose destructiveness *per se*, to counter this split subject of US nationalism with a subject whose psyche wants always and only peace. I accept that aggression is part of life and hence part of politics as well. But aggression can and must be separated from violence (violence being one form that aggression assumes), and there are ways of giving form to aggression that work in the service of democratic life, including "antagonism" and discursive conflict, strikes, civil disobedience, and even revolution. Hegel and Freud both understood that the repression of destruction can only happen by relocating destruction in the action of repression, from which it follows that any pacifism based on repression will have simply found another venue for destructiveness and in no way succeeded in its obliteration. It would further follow that the only other alternative is to find ways of crafting and checking destructiveness, giving it a livable form, which would be a way of affirming its continuing existence and assuming responsibility for the social and political forms in which it emerges. This would be a different labor than either repression or unbridled and "liberated" expression.

If I call for an overcoming of a certain schism in the national subject, it is not in the service of rehabilitating a unified and coherent subject. The subject is always outside itself, other than itself, since its relation to the other is essential to what it is (here, clearly, I remain, perversely, a Hegelian). So the following question emerges: how do we understand what it means to be a subject who is constituted in or as its relations, whose survivability is a function and effect of its modes of its relationality?

With these insights in mind, let us return to the question Asad poses to us about moral responsiveness. If just or justified violence is enacted by states, and if unjustifiable violence is enacted by non-state actors or actors opposed to existing states, then we have a way of explaining why we react to certain forms of violence with horror and to other forms with a sense of acceptance, possibly even with righteousness and triumphalism. The affective responses seem to be primary, in need of no explanation, prior to the work of understanding and interpretation. We are, as it were, against interpretation in those moments in which we react with moral horror in the face of violence. But as long as we remain against interpretation in such moments, we will not be able to give an account of why the affect of horror is differentially experienced. We will then not only proceed on the basis of this unreason, but will take it as the sign of our commendable native moral sentiment, perhaps even of our "fundamental humanity."

Paradoxically, the unreasoned schism in our responsiveness makes it impossible to react with the same horror to violence committed against all sorts of populations. In this way, when we take our moral horror to be a sign of our humanity, we fail to note that the humanity in question is, in fact, implicitly divided between those for whom we feel urgent and unreasoned concern and those whose lives and deaths simply do not touch us, or do not appear as lives at all. How are we to understand the regulatory power that creates this differential at the level of affective and moral responsiveness? Perhaps it is important to remember that responsibility requires responsiveness, and that responsiveness is not a merely subjective state, but a way of responding to what is before us with the resources that are available to us. We are already social beings, working within elaborate social interpretations both when we feel horror and when we fail to feel it at all. Our affect is never merely our own: affect is, from the start, communicated from elsewhere. It disposes us to perceive the world in a certain way, to let certain dimensions of the world in and to resist others. But if a response is always a response to a perceived state of the world, what is it that allows some aspect of the world to become perceivable and another not? How do we re-approach this question of affective response and moral evaluation by considering those already operative frameworks within which certain lives are regarded worthy of protection while others are not, precisely because they are not quite "lives" according to prevailing norms of recognizability? Affect depends upon social supports for feeling: we come to feel only in relation to a perceivable loss, one that depends on social structures of perception; and we can only feel and claim affect as our own on the condition that we have already been inscribed in a circuit of social affect.

One might, for instance, believe in the sanctity of life or adhere to a general philosophy that opposes violent action of all kinds against sentient beings, and one might invest powerful feelings in such a belief. But if certain lives are not perceivable as lives, and this includes sentient beings who are not human, then the moral prohibition against violence will be only selectively applied (and our own sentience will be only selectively mobilized). The critique of violence must begin with the question of the representability of life itself: what allows a life to become visible in its precariousness and its need for shelter, and what is it that keeps us from seeing or understanding certain lives in this way? The problem concerns the media, at the most general level, since a life can be accorded a value only on the condition that it is perceivable as a life, but it is only on the condition of certain embedded evaluative structures that a life becomes perceivable at all.

To perceive a life is not quite the same as encountering a life as precarious. Encountering a life as precarious is not a raw encounter, one in which life is stripped bare of all its usual interpretations, appearing to us outside all relations of power. An ethical attitude does not spontaneously arrive as soon as the usual interpretive frameworks are destroyed, and no pure moral conscience emerges once the shackles of everyday interpretation have been thrown off. On the contrary, it is only by challenging the dominant media that certain kinds of lives may become visible or knowable in their precariousness. It is not only or exclusively the visual apprehension of a life that forms a necessary precondition for an understanding of the precariousness of life. Another life is taken in through all the senses, if it is taken in at all. The tacit interpretive scheme that divides worthy from unworthy lives works fundamentally through the senses, differentiating the cries we can hear from those we cannot, the sights we can see from those we cannot, and likewise at the level of touch and even smell. War sustains its practices through acting on the senses, crafting them to apprehend the world selectively, deadening affect in response to certain images and sounds, and enlivening affective responses to others. This is why war works to undermine a sensate democracy, restricting what we can feel, disposing us to feel shock and outrage in the face of one expression of violence and righteous coldness in the face of another. To encounter the precariousness of another life, the senses have to be operative, which means that a struggle must be waged against those forces that seek to regulate affect in differential ways. The point is not to celebrate a full deregulation of affect, but to query the conditions of responsiveness by offering interpretive matrices for the understanding of war that question and oppose the dominant interpretations—interpretations that not only act upon affect, but take form and become effective as affect itself.

If we accept the insight that our very survival depends not on the policing of a boundary—the strategy of a certain sovereign in relation to its territory—but on recognizing how we are bound up with others, then this leads us to reconsider the way in which we conceptualize the body in the field of politics. We have to consider whether the body is rightly defined as a bounded kind of entity. What makes a body discrete is not an established morphology, as if we could identify certain bodily shapes or forms as paradigmatically human. In fact, I am not at all sure we can identify a human form, nor do I think we need to. This view has implications for rethinking gender, disability, and racialization, to name a few of the social processes that depend upon the reproduction of bodily norms. And as the critique of gender normativity, able-ism, and racist perception have made clear, there is no singular human form. We can think about demarcating the human body through identifying its boundary, or in what form it is bound, but that is to miss the crucial fact that the body is, in certain ways and even inevitably, unbound—in its acting, its receptivity, in its speech, desire, and mobility. It is outside itself, in the world of others, in a space and time it does not control, and it not only exists in the vector of these relations, but as this very vector.[11] In this sense, the body does not belong to itself.

The body, in my view, is where we encounter a range of perspectives that may or may not be our own. How I am encountered, and how I am sustained, depends fundamentally on the social and political networks in which this body lives, how I am regarded and treated, and how that regard and treatment facilitates this life or fails to make it livable. So the norms of gender through which I come to understand myself or my survivability are not made by me alone. I am already in the hands of the other when I try to take stock of who I am. I am already up against a world I never chose when I exercise my agency. It follows, then, that certain kinds of bodies will appear more precariously than others, depending on which versions of the body, or of morphology in general, support or underwrite the idea of the human life that is worth protecting, sheltering, living, mourning. These normative frameworks establish in advance what kind of life will be a life worth living, what life will be a life worth preserving, and what life will become worthy of being mourned. Such views of lives pervade and implicitly justify contemporary war. Lives are divided into those representing certain kinds of states and those representing threats to state-centered liberal democracy, so that war can then be righteously waged on behalf of some lives, while the destruction of other lives can be righteously defended.

---

11   A given morphology takes shape through a specific temporal and spatial negotiation. It is a negotiation with time in the sense that the morphology of the body does not stay the same; it ages, it changes shape, it acquires and loses capacities. And it is a negotiation with space in the sense that no body exists without existing somewhere; the body is the condition of location, and every body requires an environment to live. It would be a mistake to say that the body exists in its environment, only because the formulation is not quite strong enough. If there is no body without environment, then we cannot think the ontology of the body without the body being somewhere, without some "thereness." And here I am not trying to make an abstract point, but to consider the modes of materialization through which a body exists and by means of which that existence can be sustained and/or jeopardized.

This schism serves several functions: it constitutes the disavowal of dependency and seeks to sideline any recognition that the generalized condition of precariousness implies, socially and politically, a generalized condition of interdependency. Although not all forms of precariousness are produced by social and political arrangements, minimizing the condition of precariousness in egalitarian ways remains one task for politics. War is precisely an effort to minimize precariousness for some and to maximize it for others. Our ability to respond with outrage depends upon a tacit realization that there is a worthy life that has been injured or lost in the context of war, and no utilitarian calculus can supply the measure by which to gauge the destitution and loss of such lives. But if we are social beings and our survival depends upon a recognition of interdependency (which may not depend on the perception of likeness), then it is not as an isolated and bounded being that I survive, but as one whose boundary exposes me to others in ways that are voluntary and involuntary (sometimes at once), an exposure that is the condition of sociality and survival alike.

The boundary of who I am is the boundary of the body, but the boundary of the body never fully belongs to me. Survival depends less on the established boundary to the self than on the constitutive sociality of the body. But as much as the body, considered as social in both its surface and depth, is the condition of survival, it is also that which, under certain social conditions, imperils our lives and our survivability. Forms of physical coercion are precisely the unwilled imposition of force on bodies: being bound, gagged, forcibly exposed, ritually humiliated. We might then ask what, if anything, accounts for the survivability of those whose physical vulnerability has been exploited in this way. Of course, the fact that one's body is never fully one's own, bounded and self-referential, is the condition of passionate encounter, of desire, of longing, and of those modes of address and addressability upon which the feeling of aliveness depends. But the entire world of unwilled contact also follows from the fact that the body finds its survivability in social space and time; and this exposure or dispossession is precisely what is exploited in the case of unwilled coercion, constraint, physical injury, violence.

I would like to consider this question of survivability under conditions of war by considering briefly the recently published collection, *Poems from Guantánamo*, which includes twenty-two poems that survived the censorship of the US Department of Defense.[12] In fact, most of the poems written by Guantánamo detainees were either destroyed or confiscated, and were certainly not allowed to be passed onto the lawyers and human-rights workers who put together this slim volume. There were apparently 25,000 lines of poetry written by Shaikh Abdurraheem Muslim Dost that were destroyed by military personnel. When the Pentagon offered its rationale for the censorship, it claimed that poetry "presents a special risk" to national security because of its "content and format."[13] One has to wonder what it is about the content and format of poetry that seems so incendiary. Could it really be that the syntax or form of a poem is perceived as a threat to the security of the nation? Is it that the poems attest to the torture? Or is it that they explicitly criticize the United States, for its spurious claim to be a "protector of peace," or its irrational hatred of Islam? But since such criticisms could be made in editorials or prose, what is it about the poetry that seems particularly dangerous?

Here are two stanzas from a poem entitled "Humiliated in the Shackles," by Sami al-Haj, who was tortured at US prisons in Bagram and Kandahar before

12   Marc Falkoff, ed., *Poems from Guantánamo: The Detainees Speak*, Iowa City: University of Iowa Press, 2007.
13   Mark Falkoff, "Notes on Guantánamo," in *Poems from Guantánamo*, 4.

being transferred to Guantánamo, from where he was
recently released:

> I was humiliated in the shackles.
> How can I now compose verses? How can I now write?
> After the shackles and the nights and the suffering and
>   the Tears,
> How can I write poetry?[14]

Al-Haj attests to being tortured, and asks how he can
form words, make poetry, after such humiliation. And
yet, the very line in which he questions his ability to
make poetry is its own poetry. So the line enacts what
al-Haj cannot understand. He writes the poem, but
the poem can do no more than only openly query the
condition of its own possibility. How does a tortured
body form such words? Al-Haj is also asking how it can
be that poetry can come from a tortured body, and how
the words emerge and survive. His words move from the
condition of torture, a condition of coercion, to speech.
Is it the same body that suffers torture and that forms
the words on the page?
    The forming of those words is linked with survival,
with the capacity to survive, or survivability. Let us
remember that at the beginning of their detention,
prisoners in Guantánamo would engrave short poems on
cups they had taken away from their meals. The cups
were Styrofoam and so not only cheap, the very emblem
of cheapness, but also soft, so that prisoners would have
no access to glass or ceramics which could more easily
be used as weapons. Some would use small rocks or
pebbles to engrave their words on the cups, passing them
from cell to cell; and sometimes toothpaste was used as
a writing instrument. Apparently, as a sign of humane
treatment, they were later given paper and proper writing

---

14   Ibid., 41.

tools, but the work done with those tools was for the most part destroyed.

Some of the writings contain bitter political commentary. For instance, the opening poem by Shaker Abdurraheem Aamer:

> Peace, they say.
> Peace of mind?
> Peace on earth?
> Peace of what kind?
>
> I see them talking, arguing, fighting—
> What kind of peace are they looking for?
> Why do they kill? What are they planning?
>
> Is it just talk? Why do they argue?
> Is it so simple to kill? Is this their plan?
>
> Yes, of course!
> They talk, they argue, they kill—
> They fight for peace.[15]

It is with perspicacious irony that Aamer concludes that they "fight for peace." But what marks this poem out is the number of questions Aamer puts into poetic form, that he asks out loud, and the mixture of horror and irony in the question at the poem's center: "Is it so simple to kill?" The poem moves between confusion, horror, and irony, and concludes by exposing the hypocrisy of the US military. It focuses on the schism in the public rationality of the poet's captors: they torture in the name of peace, they kill in the name of peace. Although we do not know what the "content and format" of the censored poems might have been, this one seems to revolve around the repeated and open question, an insistent horror, a drive toward exposure.

---

15 Ibid., 20.

(Indeed, the poems make use of lyric genres that are part of Koranic scripture as well as formal features of Arab nationalist poetry, which means they are citations—so when one poet speaks, he invokes a history of speakers and at that moment establishes himself, metaphorically speaking, in their company.)

The unreasoned schism that structures the military field of affect cannot explain its own horror at the injury and loss of life sustained by those representing the legitimate nation-state, or its righteous pleasure at the humiliation and destruction of those others not organized under the sign of the nation-state. The lives of those at Guantánamo do not count as the kind of "human lives" protected by human-rights discourse. The poems themselves offer a different kind of moral responsiveness, a kind of interpretation that may, under certain conditions, contest and explode the dominant schisms running through the national and military ideology. The poems both constitute and convey a moral responsiveness to a military rationale that has restricted moral responsiveness to violence in incoherent and unjust ways. Thus we can ask: what affect is verbally conveyed by these poems, and what set of interpretations do they deliver in the form of affects, including longing and rage? The overwhelming power of mourning, loss, and isolation becomes a poetic tool of insurgency, even a challenge to individual sovereignty. Ustad Badruzzaman Badr writes:

> The whirlpool of our tears
> Is moving fast towards him
> No one can endure the power of this flood[16]

No one can endure, and yet these words arrive, as tokens of an unfathomable endurance. In a poem called "I Write My Hidden Longing," by Abdulla Majid al-Noaimi, each stanza is structured through the rhythm of suffering and appeal:

---

16 Ibid., 28.

My rib is broken, and I can find no one to heal me
My body is frail, and I can see no relief ahead[17]

But perhaps most curious are the lines in the middle of the poem in which al-Noaimi writes:

The tears of someone else's longing are affecting me
My chest cannot take the vastness of emotion[18]

Whose longing is affecting the speaker? It is someone else's longing, so that the tears seem not to be his own, or at least not exclusively his own. They belong to everyone in the camp, perhaps, or to someone else, but they impinge upon him; he finds those other feelings within him, suggesting that even in this most radical isolation, he feels what others feel. I do not know the syntax in the original Arabic, but in English "My chest cannot take the vastness of emotion" suggests that the emotion is not his alone, but of a magnitude so great that it can originate with no one person. "The tears of someone else's longing"—he is, as it were, dispossessed by these tears that are in him, but that are not exclusively his alone.

So what do these poems tell us about vulnerability and survivability? They interrogate the kinds of utterance possible at the limits of grief, humiliation, longing, and rage. The words are carved in cups, written on paper, recorded onto a surface, in an effort to leave a mark, a trace, of a living being—a sign formed by a body, a sign that carries the life of the body. And even when what happens to a body is not survivable, the words survive to say as much. This is also poetry as evidence and as appeal, in which each word is finally meant for another. The cups are passed between the cells; the poems are smuggled out of the camp. They are appeals. They are efforts to re-

---

17   Ibid., 59.
18   Ibid., 59.

establish a social connection to the world, even when there is no concrete reason to think that any such connection is possible.

In the epilogue to the collection, Ariel Dorfman compares the writings of the Guantánamo poets to those of Chilean writers under the Pinochet regime. Although clearly mindful of the ways in which the poetry conveys the conditions of the camp, Dorfman calls attention to something else about the poems:

> What I sense is that the ultimate source of these poems from Guantánamo is the simple, almost primeval, arithmetic of breathing in and out. The origin of life and the origin of language and the origin of poetry are all there, in the first breath, each breath as if it were our first, the anima, the spirit, what we inspire, what we expire, what separates us from extinction, minute after minute, what keeps us alive as we inhale and exhale the universe. And the written word is nothing more than the attempt to make that breath permanent and secure, *carve it into rock* or mark it on paper or sign it on a screen, so that its cadence will endure beyond us, outlast our breath, break the shackles of solitude, transcend our transitory body [*las cadenas precarias de la soledad*] and touch someone with its waters.[19]

---

19 *Poems*, p. 71. In the original: "Porque el origen de la vida y el origen del lenguaje y el origen de la poesía se encuentran justamente en la aritmética primigenia de la respiración; lo que aspiramos, exhalamos, inhalamos, minuto tras minuto, lo que nos mantiene vivos en un universo hostil desde el instante del nacimiento hasta el segundo anterior a nuestra extinción. Y la palabra escrita no es otra cosa que el intento de volver permanente y seguro ese aliento, marcarlo en una roca o estamparlo en un pedazo de papel o trazar su significado en una pantalla, de manera que la cadencia pueda perpetuarse más allá de nosotros, sobrevivir a lo que respiramos, romper las cadenas precarias de la soledad, trascender nuestro cuerpo transitorio y tocar a alguien con el agua de su búsqueda." *Poemas desde Guantánamo: Los detenidos hablan*, Madrid: Atalaya, 2008.

The body breathes, breathes itself into words, and finds some provisional survival there. But once the breath is made into words, the body is given over to another, in the form of an appeal. In torture, the body's vulnerability to subjection is exploited; the fact of interdependency is abused. The body that exists in its exposure and proximity to others, to external force, to all that might subjugate and subdue it, is vulnerable to injury; injury is the exploitation of that vulnerability. But this does not mean that vulnerability can be reduced to injurability. In these poems, the body is also what lives on, breathes, tries to carve its breath into stone; its breathing is precarious—it can be stopped by the force of another's torture. But if this precarious status can become the condition of suffering, it also serves the condition of responsiveness, of a formulation of affect, understood as a radical act of interpretation in the face of unwilled subjugation. The poems break through the dominant ideologies that rationalize war through recourse to righteous invocations of peace; they confound and expose the words of those who torture in the name of freedom and kill in the name of peace. In these poems we hear "the precarious cadence of solitude." This reveals two separate truths about the body: as bodies, we are exposed to others, and while this may be the condition of our desire, it also raises the possibility of subjugation and cruelty. This follows from the fact that bodies are bound up with others through material needs, through touch, through language, through a set of relations without which we cannot survive. To have one's survival bound up in such a way is a constant risk of sociality—its promise and its threat. The very fact of being bound up with others establishes the possibility of being subjugated and exploited—though in no way does it determine what political form that will take. But it also establishes the possibility of being relieved of suffering, of knowing justice and even love.

The Guantánamo poems are full of longing; they sound the incarcerated body as it makes its appeal. Its breathing is impeded, and yet it continues to breathe. The poems communicate another sense of solidarity, of interconnected lives that carry on each others' words, suffer each others' tears, and form networks that pose an incendiary risk not only to national security, but to the form of global sovereignty championed by the US. To say that the poems resist that sovereignty is not to say that they will alter the course of war or will ultimately prove more powerful than the military power of the state. But the poems clearly have political consequences—emerging from scenes of extraordinary subjugation, they remain proof of stubborn life, vulnerable, overwhelmed, their own and not their own, dispossessed, enraged, and perspicacious. As a network of transitive affects, the poems—their writing and their dissemination—are critical acts of resistance, insurgent interpretations, incendiary acts that somehow, incredibly, live through the violence they oppose, even if we do not yet know in what ways such lives will survive.

2

Torture and the Ethics of Photography: Thinking with Sontag

> Photographs state the innocence, the vulnerability of
> lives heading toward their own destruction, and this link
> between photography and death haunts all photographs
> of people.
>
> Susan Sontag, *On Photography*[1]

In *Precarious Life* (2004), I considered the question of what
it means to become ethically responsive, to consider and
attend to the suffering of others, and, more generally, of
which frames permit for the representability of the human
and which do not. Such an inquiry seems important not only
to knowing how we might respond effectively to suffering
at a distance, but also to formulating a set of precepts to
safeguard lives in their fragility and precariousness. In
this context, I am not asking about the purely subjective
sources of this kind of responsiveness.[2] Rather, I propose
to consider the way in which suffering is presented to us,
and how that presentation affects our responsiveness.
In particular, I want to understand how the *frames* that

---

1   Susan Sontag, *On Photography*, New York: Farrar, Straus and Giroux, 1977, 64.
2   Judith Butler, *Giving an Account of Oneself*, New York: Fordham University
Press, 2005.

allocate the recognizability of certain figures of the human are themselves linked with broader *norms* that determine what will and will not be a grievable life. My point, which is hardly new but bears repeating, is that whether and how we respond to the suffering of others, how we formulate moral criticisms, how we articulate political analyses, depends upon a certain field of perceptible reality having already been established. This field of perceptible reality is one in which the notion of the recognizable human is formed and maintained over and against what cannot be named or regarded as the human—a figure of the non-human that negatively determines and potentially unsettles the recognizably human.

At the time *Precarious Life* was written, the tortures at Abu Ghraib had not yet come to light. I was working with only the pictures of the shackled and crouched bodies in Guantánamo Bay, knowing neither the details of torture nor of other linked representational issues, such as the debates about showing the war dead in Iraq and the problem of "embedded reporting." Throughout the Bush regime, we saw a concerted effort on the part of the state to regulate the visual field. The phenomenon of embedded reporting came to the fore with the invasion of Iraq in March 2003, when it seemed to be defined as an arrangement whereby journalists agreed to report only from the perspective established by military and governmental authorities. "Embedded" journalists traveled only on certain transports, looked only at certain scenes, and relayed home images and narratives of only certain kinds of action. Embedded reporting implies that reporters working under such conditions agree not to make the mandating of perspective *itself* into a topic to be reported and discussed; hence these reporters were offered access to the war only on the condition that their gaze remain restricted to the established parameters of designated action.

Embedded reporting has taken place in less explicit ways as well. One clear example is the media's agreement not to show pictures of the war dead, our own or their own, on the grounds that that it undermined the war effort and jeopardized the nation. Journalists and newspapers were actively denounced for showing coffins of the American war dead shrouded in flags. Such images were not to be seen in case they aroused certain kinds of negative sentiment.[3] This mandating of what can be seen—a concern with regulating content—was supplemented by control over the perspective according to which the action and destruction of war could be seen at all. By regulating perspective in addition to content, the state authorities were clearly interested in regulating the visual modes of participation in the war. Seeing was tacitly understood as linked with the occupation of a position and, indeed, a certain disposition of the subject itself. A second place in which embedded reporting implicitly occurred was in the Abu Ghraib photographs. The camera angle, the frame, the posed subjects, all suggest that those who took the photographs were actively involved in the perspective of the war, elaborating that perspective, crafting, commending, and validating a point of view.

In her final book, *Regarding the Pain of Others*, Susan Sontag remarks that this practice of embedded reporting begins some twenty years earlier, with the coverage of the British Campaign in the Falklands in 1982, when only two photojournalists were permitted to enter the region and

3   Bill Carter, "Pentagon Ban on Pictures Of Dead Troops Is Broken," *New York Times*, April 23, 2004; Helen Thomas, "Pentagon Manages War Coverage By Limiting Coffin Pictures," *The Boston Channel*, October 29, 2003; Patrick Barrett, "US TV Blackout Hits Litany of War Dead," *Guardian*, April 30, 2004, http://www.guardian.co.uk/media/2004/apr/30/Iraqandthemedia.usnews; National Security Archive, "Return of The Fallen," April 28, 2005, http://www.gwu.edu/~nsarchiv/NSAEBB/NSAEBB152/index.htm; Dana Milbank, "Curtains Ordered for Media Coverage of Returning Coffins," *Washington Post*, October 21, 2003; Sheryl Gay Stolberg, "Senate Backs Ban on Photos Of G.I. Coffins," *New York Times*, June 22, 2004, http://query.nytimes.com/gst/fullpage.html?res=990DE2DB1339F931A15755C0A9629C8B63

no television broadcasts were allowed.[4] Since that time, journalists have increasingly agreed to comply with the exigencies of embedded reporting in order to secure access to the action itself. But what is the action to which access is thus secured? In the case of the recent and current wars, the visual perspective that the US Department of Defense permitted to the media actively structured our cognitive apprehension of the war. And although restricting how or what we see is not exactly the same as dictating a storyline, it is a way of interpreting in advance what will and will not be included in the field of perception. The very action of the war, its practices and its effects, are meant to be established by the perspective that the Department of Defense orchestrates and permits, thereby illustrating the orchestrative power of the state to ratify what will be called reality: the extent of what is perceived to exist.

The regulation of perspective thus suggests that the frame can conduct certain kinds of interpretations. In my view, it does not make sense to accept Sontag's claim, made repeatedly throughout her writings, that the photograph cannot by itself offer an interpretation, that we need captions and written analysis to supplement the discrete and punctual image. In her view, the image can only affect us, not provide us with an understanding of what we see. But although Sontag is clearly right to maintain that we need captions and analyses, her claim that the photograph is not itself an interpretation nevertheless leads us into a different bind. She writes that whereas both prose and painting can be interpretive, photography is merely "selective," suggesting that it gives us a partial "imprint" of reality: "while a painting, even one that achieves photographic standards of resemblance, is never more than the stating of an interpretation, a photograph is never less than an emanation (light waves reflected by

---

4   Susan Sontag, *Regarding the Pain of Others*, New York: Farrar, Straus and Giroux, 2003, 65.

objects)—a material vestige of its subject in a way that no painting can be."[5]

Sontag argued that although photographs have the capacity momentarily to move us, they do not allow the building up of an interpretation. If a photograph becomes effective in informing or moving us politically, it is, in her view, only because the image is received within the context of a relevant political consciousness. For Sontag, photographs render truths in a dissociated moment; they "flash up" in a Benjaminian sense, and so provide only fragmented or dissociated imprints of reality. As a result, they are always atomic, punctual, and discrete. What photographs lack is narrative coherence, and it is such coherence alone, in her view, that satisfies the needs of the understanding (a strange twist on a fundamentally Kantian position).[6] Nonetheless, while narrative coherence might be a standard for some sorts of interpretation, it is surely not so for all. Indeed, if the notion of a "visual interpretation" is not to become oxymoronic, it seems important to acknowledge that, in framing reality, the photograph has already determined what will count within the frame— and this act of delimitation is surely interpretive, as are, potentially, the various effects of angle, focus, light, etc.

In my view, interpretation is not to be conceived restrictively in terms of a subjective act. Rather, interpretation takes place by virtue of the structuring constraints of genre and form on the communicability of affect—and so sometimes takes place against one's will or, indeed, in spite of oneself. Thus, it is not just that the photographer and/or the viewer actively and deliberately interpret, but that the photograph itself becomes a structuring scene of interpretation—and one that may unsettle both maker and viewer in its turn. It would not be quite right to reverse

5   Ibid., 6, 154.
6   We can see Sontag the writer here differentiating her trade from that of the photographers with whom she surrounded herself in the last decades of her life.

the formulation completely and say that the photograph interprets us (although some photographs, especially those of war, may do that), since that formulation keeps the metaphysics of the subject intact, even as it reverses the assigned positions. And yet, photographs do act on us. The specific question that concerned Sontag, however, in both *On Photography* and *Regarding the Pain of Others*, was whether photographs still had the power—or ever did have the power—to communicate the suffering of others in such a way that viewers might be prompted to alter their political assessment of war. For photographs to communicate effectively in this way, they must have a transitive function: they must act upon viewers in ways that have a direct bearing on the kinds of judgments those viewers will formulate about the world. Sontag concedes that photographs are transitive. They do not merely portray or represent—they relay affect. In fact, in times of war, this transitive affectivity of the photograph may overwhelm and numb its viewers. She is, though, less convinced that a photograph might motivate its viewers to change their point of view or to assume a new course of action.

In the late 1970s, Sontag argued that the photographic image had lost the power to enrage, to incite. She claimed in *On Photography* that the visual representation of suffering had become clichéd, and that as a result of being bombarded with sensationalist photography our capacity for ethical responsiveness had been diminished. In her reconsideration of this thesis twenty-six years later, in *Regarding the Pain of Others*, Sontag is more ambivalent about the status of the photograph which, she concedes, can and must represent human suffering, establishing through the visual frame a proximity that keeps us alert to the human cost of war, famine, and destruction in places that may be distant both geographically and culturally. In order for photographs to evoke a moral response, they must not only maintain the capacity to shock, but also appeal to our sense of moral obligation. Although Sontag never thought that "shock" was particularly instructive, she nevertheless laments that photography has lost its capacity in this regard. In her view, shock itself had become a kind of cliché, and contemporary photography tended to aestheticize suffering for the purposes of satisfying a consumer demand—this last function making it inimical to ethical responsiveness and political interpretation alike.

In this last book, Sontag still faults photography for not being writing: it lacks narrative continuity and remains fatally linked to the momentary. Photographs cannot produce ethical pathos in us, she remarks; or if they do, it is only momentarily—we see something atrocious and move on at a moment's notice. The pathos conveyed by narrative forms, by contrast, "does not wear out". "Narratives can make us understand: photographs do something else. They haunt us."[7] Is she right? Is she correct to suggest that narratives do not haunt, and that photographs fail to make us understand? To the extent that photographs convey affect, they seem to invoke a kind of responsiveness that threatens the only model of understanding Sontag trusts. Indeed, despite the overwhelming power of the photograph of napalm burning on the skins of the crying, running children during the Vietnam war (an image whose force she acknowledges), Sontag maintains that "a narrative seems more likely to be effective than an image" in helping to mobilize us effectively against a war.[8]

Interestingly, although narratives might mobilize us, photographs are needed as evidence for war crimes. In fact, Sontag argues that the contemporary notion of atrocity requires photographic evidence: if there is no photographic evidence, there is no atrocity. But if this is the case, then the photograph is built into the notion of atrocity, and

---

7   Ibid., 83.
8   Ibid., 122.

photographic evidence establishes the truth of the claim of atrocity in the sense that photographic evidence has become all but obligatory to demonstrate the fact of atrocity— which means that in this instance photography is built into the case made for truth, or that there can be no truth without photography. Sontag would doubtless rejoin that the judgment whether an atrocity has taken place is a kind of interpretation, verbal or narrative, that seeks recourse to the photograph to substantiate its claim. But this is a problematic response for at least two reasons: first, the photograph builds the evidence and, so, the claim; second, Sontag's position misunderstands the way that non-verbal or non-linguistic media make their "arguments." Even the most transparent of documentary images is framed, and framed for a purpose, carrying that purpose within its frame and implementing it through the frame. If we take such a purpose to be interpretive, then it would appear that the photograph still interprets the reality it registers, and this dual function is preserved even when it is offered as "evidence" for another interpretation presented in written or verbal form. After all, rather than merely referring to acts of atrocity, the photograph builds and confirms these acts for those who would name them as such.

For Sontag there is something of a persistent split between being affected and being able to think and understand, a split represented in the differing effects of photography and prose. She writes that "sentiment is more likely to crystallize around a photograph than around a verbal slogan," and doubtless sentiment can crystallize without affecting our capacity to understand events or to take up a course of action in response to them.[9] But in Sontag's view, when sentiment crystallizes, it forestalls thinking. Moreover, the sentiment crystallizes not around the event photographed, but around the photographic image itself. In fact, Sontag's concern is that the photograph substitutes

9   Ibid., 85.

for the event to such an extent that it structures memory more effectively than either understanding or narrative.[10] The problem is less with the "loss of reality" this entails (the photograph still registers the real, if obliquely), but with the triumph of a fixed sentiment over more clearly cognitive capacities.

For our purposes, though, we need only consider that the mandated visual image produced by "embedded reporting," the one that complies with state and Defense Department requirements, builds an interpretation. We can even say that what Sontag calls "the political consciousness" motivating the photographer to yield up the compliant photograph is to some extent structured by the photograph itself, even embedded in the frame. We do not have to be supplied with a caption or a narrative in order to understand that a political background is being explicitly formulated and renewed through and by the frame, that the frame functions not only as a boundary to the image, but as structuring the image itself. If the image in turn structures how we register reality, then it is bound up with the interpretive scene in which we operate. The question for war photography thus concerns not only what it shows, but also how it shows what it shows. The "how" not only organizes the image, but works to organize our perception and thinking as well. If state power attempts to regulate a perspective that reporters and cameramen are there to confirm, then the action of perspective in and as the frame is part of the interpretation of the war compelled by the state. The photograph is not merely a visual image awaiting interpretation; it is itself actively interpreting, sometimes forcibly so.

As a visual interpretation, the photograph can only be conducted within certain kinds of lines and so within certain kinds of frames—unless, of course, the mandatory framing becomes part of the story; unless there is a way to photograph the frame itself. At that point, the photograph

---

10   Ibid., 89.

that yields its frame to interpretation thereby opens up to critical scrutiny the restrictions on interpreting reality. It exposes and thematizes the mechanism of restriction, and constitutes a disobedient act of seeing. The point is not to engage in hyper-reflexivity, but to consider what forms of social and state power are "embedded" in the frame, including state and military regulatory regimes. Rarely does this operation of mandatory and dramaturgical "framing" become part of what is seen, much less of what is told. But when it does, we are led to interpret the interpretation that has been imposed upon us, developing our analysis into a social critique of regulatory and censorious power.

If Sontag were right about the photograph no longer having the power to excite and enrage us in such a way that we might change our political views and conducts, then Donald Rumsfeld's response to the photos depicting the torture in the Abu Ghraib prison would not have made sense. When, for instance, Rumsfeld claimed that publishing the photos of torture and humiliation and rape would allow them "to define us as Americans," he attributed to photography an enormous power to construct national identity itself.[11] The photographs would not just show something atrocious, but would make our capacity to commit atrocity into a defining concept of American identity.

Recent war photography departs significantly from the conventions of war photojournalism that were at work thirty or forty years ago, where the photographer or camera person would attempt to enter the action through angles and modes of access that sought to expose the war in ways that no government had planned. Now, the state works on the field of perception and, more generally, the field of representability, in order to control affect—in anticipation of the way affect is not only structured by interpretation, but structures interpretation as well. What is at stake

---

11   Donald Rumsfeld, CNN, May 8, 2004.

is the regulation of those images that might galvanize political opposition to a war. I refer to "representability" here, rather than "representation," because this field is structured by state permission (or, rather, the state seeks to establish control over it, if always with only partial success). As a result, we cannot understand the field of representability simply by examining its explicit contents, since it is constituted fundamentally by what is left out, maintained outside the frame within which representations appear. We can think of the frame, then, as active, as both jettisoning and presenting, and as doing both at once, in silence, without any visible sign of its operation. What emerges under these conditions is a viewer who assumes him or herself to be in an immediate (and incontestable) visual relation to reality.

The operation of the frame, where state power exercises its forcible dramaturgy, is not normally representable— and when it is, it risks becoming insurrectionary and hence subject to state punishment and control. Prior to the events and actions represented within the frame, there is an active if unmarked delimitation of the field itself, and so of a set of contents and perspectives that are never shown, that it becomes impermissible to show. These constitute the non-thematized background of what is represented and are thus one of its absent organizing features. They can be approached only by thematizing the delimiting function itself, thereby exposing the forcible dramaturgy of the state in collaboration with those who deliver the visual news of the war by complying with the permissible perspectives. That delimiting is part of an operation of power that does not appear as a figure of oppression. To imagine the state as a dramaturge, thus representing its power through an anthropomorphic figure, would be mistaken, since it is essential to its continuing operation that this power should not be seen and, indeed, should not be organized (or figured) as the action of a subject. Rather, it is precisely a non-figurable and, to some extent,

non-intentional operation of power that works to delimit
the domain of representability itself. However, that such
a form of power is non-figurable as an intentional subject
does not mean that it cannot be marked or shown. On
the contrary, what is shown when it comes into view is
the staging apparatus itself, the maps that exclude certain
regions, the directives of the army, the positioning of the
cameras, the punishments that lie in wait if reporting
protocols are breached.

But when one does see the framing of the frame, what is
it that is going on? I would suggest that the problem here
is not just internal to the life of the media, but involves the
structuring effects that certain larger norms, themselves
often racializing and civilizational, have on what is
provisionally called "reality."

Before the publication of the photos from Abu Ghraib,
I had sought to relate three different terms in my effort
to understand the visual dimension of war as it relates to
the question of whose lives are grievable and whose are
not. In the first instance, there are norms, explicit or tacit,
governing which human lives count as human and as
living, and which do not. These norms are determined to
some degree by the question of when and where a life is
grievable and, correlatively, when and where the loss of a
life remains ungrievable and unrepresentable. This stark
formulation is not intended to exclude those lives that are
at once grieved and ungrieved, that are marked as lost
but are not fully recognizable as a loss, such as the lives
of those who live with war as an intangible yet persistent
background of everyday life.

These broad social and political norms operate in
many ways, one of which involves frames that govern the
perceptible, that exercise a delimiting function, bringing
an image into focus on condition that some portion of the
visual field is ruled out. The represented image thereby
signifies its admissibility into the domain of representability,

and thus at the same time signifies the delimiting function of the frame—even as, or precisely because, it does not represent it. In other words, the image, which is supposed to deliver reality, in fact withdraws reality from perception.

In the public discourse on Guantánamo Bay, the police harassment of Arabs in the US (both Arab-Americans and those with visas or green cards), and the suspension of civil liberties, certain norms have been operative in establishing who is human and so entitled to human rights and who is not. Implicit in this discourse of humanization is the question of grievability: whose life, if extinguished, would be publicly grievable and whose life would leave either no public trace to grieve, or only a partial, mangled, and enigmatic trace? If, as I have argued, norms are enacted through visual and narrative frames, and framing presupposes decisions or practices that leave substantial losses outside the frame, then we have to consider that full inclusion and full exclusion are not the only options. Indeed, there are deaths that are partially eclipsed and partially marked, and that instability may well activate the frame, making the frame itself unstable. So the point would not be to locate what is "in" or "outside" the frame, but what vacillates between those two locations, and what, foreclosed, becomes encrypted in the frame itself.

Norms and frames constitute the first two hinges for my analysis; the last of the three is suffering itself. It would be a mistake to take this as exclusively or paradigmatically human suffering. It is precisely as human animals that humans suffer. And in the context of war, one could, and surely should, point to the destruction of animals, of habitats, and of other conditions for sentient life, citing the toxic effects of war munitions on natural environments and ecosystems, and the condition of creatures who may survive but have been saturated in poisons. The point, however, would not be to catalog the forms of life damaged by war, but to reconceive life itself as a set of largely unwilled interdependencies, even systemic relations, which imply

that the "ontology" of the human is not separable from
the "ontology" of the animal. It is not just a question of
two categories that overlap, but of a co-constitution that
implies the need for a reconceptualization of the ontology
of life itself.[12]

How does one object to human suffering without
perpetuating a form of anthropocentrism that has so
readily been used for destructive purposes? Do I need
to make plain in what I consider the human to consist? I
propose that we consider the way "the human" works as
a differential norm: Let us think of the human as a value
and a morphology that may be allocated and retracted,
aggrandized, personified, degraded and disavowed,
elevated and affirmed. The norm continues to produce the
nearly impossible paradox of a human who is no human,
or of the human who effaces the human as it is otherwise
known. Wherever there is the human, there is the
inhuman; when we now proclaim as human some group
of beings who have previously not been considered to be,
in fact, human, we admit that the claim to "humanness" is
a shifting prerogative. Some humans take their humanness
for granted, while others struggle to gain access to it. The
term "human" is constantly doubled, exposing the ideality
and coercive character of the norm: some humans qualify
as human; some humans do not. When I use the term
in the second of these clauses, I do nothing more than
assert a discursive life for a human who does not embody
the norm that determines what and who will count as a
human life. When Donna Haraway asks whether we ever
become human, she is at once positing a "we" outside the
norm of the human, and questioning whether the human
is ever something that can be fully accomplished.[13] I would
suggest that this norm is not something that we must seek

---

12   Cf. Haraway, *The Companion Species Manifesto.*
13   Haraway offered this question at the Avenali Lecture at the University of
California at Berkeley, September 16, 2003.

to embody, but a differential of power that we must learn to read, to assess culturally and politically, and to oppose in its differential operations. And yet, we also need the term, in order to assert it precisely where it cannot be asserted, and to do this in the name of opposing the differential of power by which it operates, as a way of working against the forces of neutralization or erasure that separate us from knowing and responding to the suffering that is caused, sometimes in our names.

If, as the philosopher Emmanuel Levinas claims, it is the face of the other that demands from us an ethical response, then it would seem that the norms that would allocate who is and is not human arrive in visual form. These norms work to *give face* and to *efface*. Accordingly, our capacity to respond with outrage, opposition, and critique will depend in part on how the differential norm of the human is communicated through visual and discursive frames. There are ways of framing that will bring the human into view in its frailty and precariousness, that will allow us to stand for the value and dignity of human life, to react with outrage when lives are degraded or eviscerated without regard for their value as lives. And then there are frames that foreclose responsiveness, where this activity of foreclosure is effectively and repeatedly performed by the frame itself—its own negative action, as it were, toward what will not be explicitly represented. For alternative frames to exist and permit another kind of content would perhaps communicate a suffering that might lead to an alteration of our political assessment of the current wars. For photographs to communicate in this way, they must have a transitive function, making us susceptible to ethical responsiveness.

How do the norms that govern which lives will be regarded as human enter into the frames through which discourse and visual representation proceed, and how do these in turn delimit or orchestrate our ethical responsiveness to suffering? I am not suggesting that these norms determine our responses, such that the latter are reduced to behaviorist effects of a monstrously powerful visual culture. I am suggesting only that the way these norms enter into frames and into larger circuits of communicability are vigorously contestable precisely because the effective regulation of affect, outrage, and ethical response is at stake.

I want to suggest that the Abu Ghraib photographs neither numb our senses nor determine a particular response. This has to do with the fact that they occupy no single time and no specific space. They are shown again and again, transposed from context to context, and this history of their successive framing and reception conditions, without determining, the kinds of public interpretations of torture we have. In particular, the norms governing the "human" are relayed and abrogated through the communication of these photos; the norms are not thematized as such, but they broker the encounter between first-world viewers who seek to understand "what happened over there" and this visual "trace" of the human in a condition of torture. This trace does not tell us what the human is, but it provides evidence that a break from the norm governing the subject of rights has taken place and that something called "humanity" is at issue here. The photo cannot restore integrity to the body it registers. The visual trace is surely not the same as the full restitution of the humanity of the victim, however desirable that obviously is. The photograph, shown and circulated, becomes the public condition under which we feel outrage and construct political views to incorporate and articulate that outrage.

I have found Susan Sontag's last publications to be good company as I consider what the photos of torture are and what they do, including both her *Regarding the Pain of Others* and "Regarding the Torture of Others," which was released on the internet and published in the *New York Times* after the release of the Abu Ghraib photographs.[14] The photos showed brutality,

---

14   Sontag, "Regarding The Torture Of Others," *New York Times*, May 23, 2004, http://www.nytimes.com/2004/05/23/magazine/23PRISONS.html

humiliation, rape, murder, and in that sense were clear representational evidence of war crimes. They have functioned in many ways, including as evidence in legal proceedings against those pictured as engaging in acts of torture and humiliation. They have also become iconic for the way that the US government, in alliance with Britain, spurned the Geneva Conventions, in particular the protocols governing the fair treatment of prisoners of war. It quickly became clear in the months of April and May 2004 that there was a pattern to the photographs and that, as the Red Cross had contended for many months before the scandal broke, there was a systematic mistreatment of prisoners in Iraq, paralleling a systematic mistreatment at Guantánamo.[15] Only later did it become clear that protocols devised for Guantánamo had been deployed by the personnel at Abu Ghraib, and that both sets of protocols were indifferent to the Geneva accords. The question of whether governmental officials called what is depicted in the photos "abuse" or "torture" suggests that the relation to international law is already at work; abuse can be addressed by disciplinary proceedings within the military, but torture is a war crime, actionable within international courts. They did not dispute that the photographs are real, that they record something that actually happened. Establishing the referentiality of the photographs was, however, not enough. The photos are not only shown, but named; the way that they are shown, the way they are framed, and the words used to describe what is shown, work together to produce an interpretive matrix for what is seen.

---

15   Geoffrey Miller, Major General in the US Army, is generally regarded as responsible for devising the torture protocols at Guantánamo, including the use of dogs, and for transposing those protocols to Abu Ghraib. See Joan Walsh, "The Abu Ghraib Files," *Salon.com*, March 14, 2006, http://www.salon. com/news/abu_ghraib/2006/03/14/introduction/index.html; see also Andy Worthington, *The Guantánamo Files: The Stories of the 774 Detainees in America's Illegal Prison*, London: Pluto Press, 2007.

But before we consider briefly the conditions under which they were published and the form in which they were made public, let us consider the way the frame works to establish a relation between the photographer, the camera, and the scene. The photos depict or represent a scene, the visual image preserved within the photographic frame. But the frame also belongs to a camera that is situated spatially in the field of vision, thus not shown within the image, though still functioning as the technological precondition of an image, and indicated indirectly by the camera. Although the camera is outside the frame, it is clearly "in" the scene as its constitutive outside. When the photographing of these acts of torture becomes a topic of public debate, the scene of the photograph is extended. The scene becomes not just the spatial location and social scenario in the prison itself, but the entire social sphere in which the photograph is shown, seen, censored, publicized, discussed, and debated. So we might say that the scene of the photograph has changed through time.

Let us notice a few things about this larger scene, one in which visual evidence and discursive interpretation play off against one another. There was "news" because there were photos, the photos laid claim to a representational status, and traveled beyond the original place where they were taken, the place depicted in the photos themselves. On the one hand, they are referential; on the other, they change their meaning depending on the context in which they are shown and the purpose for which they are invoked. The photos were published on the internet and in newspapers, but in both venues selections were made: some photos were shown, others were not; some were large, others small. For a long time, *Newsweek* retained possession of numerous photos that it refused to publish on the grounds that doing so would not be "useful." Useful for what purpose? Clearly, they meant "useful to the war effort"—surely they did not mean "useful for individuals who require free access to information about the current war in order to establish lines of accountability and to form political viewpoints on that war." In restricting what we may see, do the government and the media not then also limit the kinds of evidence the public has at its disposal, to make judgments about the wisdom and course of the war? If, as Sontag claims, the contemporary notion of atrocity requires photographic evidence, then the only way to establish that torture has taken place is through presenting such evidence, at which point the evidence constitutes the phenomenon. And yet, within a frame of potential or actual legal proceedings the photo is already framed within the discourse of law and of truth.

In the US, the prurient interest in the photographs themselves seemed to preempt a fair amount of political response. The photo of Lynndie England with the leash around a man's head was front and center in the *New York Times*; yet other papers relegated it to the inside pages, depending on whether they sought a more or less incendiary presentation. Within military court proceedings, the photo is considered evidence from within a frame of potential or actual legal proceedings and is already framed within the discourse of law and of truth. The photo presupposes a photographer—a person never shown in the frame. The question of guilt has been restricted to the juridical question of who committed the acts, or of who was ultimately responsible for those who did commit them. And the prosecutions have been limited to the most well-publicized cases.

It took some time before the question was raised as to who actually took the photos, and what could be inferred from their occluded spatial relation to the images themselves.[16] Did they take them in order to expose the abuse, or to gloat in the spirit of US triumphalism? Was the taking of the photo a way to participate in the event and, if so, in what way? It would seem that the photos were taken as

---

16   A key exception is the excellent film, *Standard Operating Procedure,* dir. Errol Morris, 2008.

records, producing, as the *Guardian* put it, a pornography of the event[17]—but at some point, someone, or perhaps several people, aware now of a potential investigation, realized that there was something wrong with what the photos depicted. It may be that the photographers were ambivalent at the time they took the photos or that they became ambivalent in retrospect; it may be that they feasted on the sadistic scene in some way that would invite a psychological explanation. Although I would not dispute the importance of psychology for understanding such behavior, I do not think it should be used to reduce torture exclusively to individual pathological acts. Since we are clearly confronted with a group scene in these photographs, we need something more like a psychology of group behavior, or, better yet, an account of how the norms of war in this instance neutralized morally significant relationships to violence and injurability. And since we are also in a specific political situation, any effort to reduce the acts to individual psychologies alone would return us to familiar problems with the notion of the individual or the person conceived as the causal matrix for the understanding of events. Considering the structural and spatial dynamics of the photograph offers an alternative point of departure for understanding how the norms of war are operating in these events—and even how individuals are taken up by these norms and, in turn, take them up.

The photographer is recording a visual image of the scene, approaching it through a frame before which those involved in the torture and its triumphal aftermath also stood and posed. The relation between the photographer and the photographed takes place by virtue of the frame. The frame permits, orchestrates, and mediates that relation. And though the photographers at Abu Ghraib had no Defense Department authorization for the pictures

---

17   Joanna Bourke, "Torture as Pornography," *Guardian*, May 7, 2004, http://www.guardian.co.uk/world/2004/may/07/gender.uk

they took, perhaps their perspective can also rightly be considered a form of embedded reporting. After all, their perspective on the so-called enemy was not idiosyncratic, but shared—so widely shared, it seems, that there was hardly a thought that something might be amiss here. Can we see these photographers not only as reiterating and confirming a certain practice of decimating Islamic cultural practice and norms, but as conforming to—and articulating—the widely shared social norms of the war?

So what are the norms according to which soldiers and security personnel, actively recruited from private firms contracted to supervise prisons in the US, acted as they did? And what are the norms that reside in the active framing by the camera, since these form the basis of the cultural and political text at issue here? If the photograph not only depicts, but also builds on and augments the event—if the photograph can be said to reiterate and continue the event—then it does not strictly speaking postdate the event, but becomes crucial to its production, its legibility, its illegibility, and its very status as reality. Perhaps the camera promises a festive cruelty: "Oh, good, the camera's here: let's begin the torture so that the photograph can capture and commemorate our act!" If so, the photograph is already at work prompting, framing, and orchestrating the act, even as it captures the act at the moment of its accomplishment.

The task, in a way, is to understand the operation of a norm circumscribing a reality that works through the action of the frame itself; we have yet to understand this frame, these frames, where they come from and what kind of action they perform. Given that there is more than one photographer, and that we cannot clearly discern their motivation from the photos that are available, we are left to read the scene in another way. We can say with some confidence that the photographer is catching or recording the event, but this only raises the issue of the implied audience. It may be that he or she records the event in order to replay the images to those perpetrating the torture, so they can enjoy the reflection of their actions on the digital camera and disseminate their particular accomplishment quickly. The photos may also be understood as a kind of evidence, conceived as proof that just punishment was administered. As an action, taking a photograph is neither always anterior to the event, nor always posterior to it. The photograph is a kind of promise that the event will continue, indeed it is that very continuation, producing an equivocation at the level of the temporality of the event: Did those actions happen then? Do they continue to happen? Does the photograph continue the event into the future?

It would seem that photographing the scene is a way of contributing to it, providing it with a visual reflection and documentation, giving it the status of history in some sense. Does the photograph or, indeed, the photographer, contribute to the scene? Act upon the scene? Intervene upon the scene? Photography has a relation to intervention, but photographing is not the same as intervening. There are photos of bodies bound together, of individuals killed, of forced fellatio, of dehumanizing degradation, and they were taken unobstructed. The field of vision is clear. No one is seen lunging in front of the camera to intercept the view. No one is shackling the photographer and throwing him or her in jail for participating in a crime. This is torture in plain view, in front of the camera, even for the camera. It is centered action, with the torturers regularly turning toward the camera to make sure their own faces are shown, even as the faces of the tortured are mainly shrouded. The camera itself is ungagged, unbound, and so occupies and references the safety zone that surrounds and supports the persecutors in the scene. We do not know how much of the torture was consciously performed for the camera, as a way of showing what the US can do, as a sign of its military triumphalism, demonstrating its ability to effect a complete degradation of the putative enemy, in an effort to win the clash of civilizations and subject the ostensible barbarians to our civilizing mission which, as we can see, has rid itself so beautifully of its own barbarism. But to the extent that the photograph communicates the scene, potentially, to newspapers and media sources, the torture is, in some sense, *for* the camera; it is from the start meant to be communicated. Its own perspective is in plain view, and the cameraman or woman is referenced by the smiles that the torturers offer him, as if to say, "thank you for taking my picture, thank you for memorializing my triumph." And then there is the question of whether the photographs were shown to those who might yet be tortured, as a warning and a threat. It is clear they were used to blackmail those depicted with the threat that their families would see their humiliation and shame, especially sexual shame.

The photograph depicts—it has a representational and referential function. But at least two questions follow. The first has to do with what the referential function does, besides simply referring: what other functions does it serve? What other effects does it produce? The second, which I will deal with below, has to do with the range of what is represented. If the photo represents reality, which reality is it that is represented? And how does the frame circumscribe what will be called reality in this instance?

If we are to identify war crimes within the conduct of war, then the "business of war" itself is ostensibly something other than the war crime (we cannot, within such a framework, talk about the "crime of war"). But what if the war crimes amount to an enactment of the very norms that serve to legitimate the war? The Abu Ghraib photos are surely referential, but can we tell in what way the photos not only register the norms of war, but also came to constitute the visual emblem of the war in Iraq? When the business of war is subject to the omnipresence of stray cameras, time and space can be randomly chronicled and recorded, and future and external perspectives come to inhere in the scene itself. But the efficacy of the camera works along a temporal trajectory other than the chronology it secures.

The visual archive circulates. The date function on the camera may specify precisely when the event happened, but the indefinite circulability of the image allows the event to continue to happen and, indeed, thanks to these images, the event has not stopped happening.

It was difficult to understand the proliferation of images, but it seemed to coincide with a proliferation of acts, a frenzy of photography. There is not only a certain pleasure involved in the scenes of torture, something we must consider, but also a pleasure, or perhaps a compulsion, involved in the act of taking the photographs itself. Why else would there be so many? Joanna Bourke, an historian at Birkbeck College who published a book about the history of rape, wrote an article in the *Guardian* on May 7, 2003 entitled "Torture as Pornography."[18] Bourke uses "pornography" as an explanatory category to account for the role of the camera as actor in the scene. She writes, shrewdly, that one senses an exultation in the photographer, though since there are no images of the latter, Bourke draws her conclusion from considering the photographs, their number, and the circumstances of their taking:

> the people taking the photographs exult in the genitals of their victims. There is no moral confusion here: the photographers don't even seem aware that they are recording a war crime. There is no suggestion that they are documenting anything particularly morally skewed. For the person behind the camera, the aesthetic of pornography protects them from blame.[19]

So perhaps I am odd, but as I understand it, *pace* Bourke, the problem with the photos is *not* that one person is exulting in another person's genitals. Let's assume that we all do that on occasion and that there is nothing particularly

18   Ibid.
19   Ibid.

objectionable in that exultation, and that it may even be precisely what is needed to make for a good time. What is clearly objectionable, however, is the use of coercion and the exploitation of sexual acts in the service of shaming and debasing another human being. The distinction is crucial, of course, since the first objection finds the sexuality of the exchange to be a problem, while the second identifies the problem in the coercive nature of sexual acts. This equivocation was compounded when President Bush emerged from the Senate chambers after viewing some of the photographs. When asked for his response he replied, "it is disgusting," leaving it unclear as to whether he was referring to the homosexual acts of sodomy and fellatio or to the physically coercive and psychologically debasing conditions and effects of the torture itself.[20] Indeed, if it was the homosexual acts that he found "disgusting," then he had clearly missed the point about torture, having allowed his sexual revulsion and moralism to take the place of an ethical objection. But if it was the torture that was disgusting, then why did he use that word, rather than *wrong* or *objectionable* or *criminal*? The word "disgusting" keeps the equivocation intact, leaving two issues questionably intertwined: homosexual acts on the one hand, and physical and sexual torture on the other.

In some ways, the faulting of these photographs as pornography seems to commit a similar category mistake. Bourke's conjectures on the psychology of the photographer are interesting, and there is doubtless some mix of cruelty and pleasure here that we need to think about.[21] But how would we go about deciding the issue? Don't we need to ask why we are prepared to believe that these affective dispositions are the operative motivations in

---

20   *New York Times*, May 1, 2004, http://query.nytimes.com/gst/fullpage. html?res=9502E0DB153DF932A35756C0A9629C8B63

21   See *Standard Operating Procedure*, as well as Linda Williams, "The Forcible Frame: Errol Morris's *Standard Operating Procedure*" (*courtesy of the author*).

order to approach the question of photography and torture critically? How would the photographer's awareness that he or she is recording a war crime appear within the terms of the photograph itself? It is one thing to affirm that some of what is recorded is rape and torture, and another to say that the means of representation is pornographic. My fear is that the old slippage from pornography to rape reappears here in unexamined form. The view was that pornography motivates or incites rape, that it is causally linked with rape (those who watch it end up doing it), and that what happens at the level of the body in rape happens at the level of representation in pornography.[22]

There seems to be no sense that the photographs, at the time they were taken, are intervening as an instrument of moral inquiry, political exposure, or legal investigation. The soldiers and security personnel photographed are clearly at ease with the camera, indeed playing to it, and although I have suggested that there might be an element of triumphalism, Bourke herself claims that the photographs act as "souvenirs." She further argues that the abuse is performed for the camera, and it is this thesis—which I tentatively share—that leads her to a conclusion with which I disagree. Her argument is that the abuse is performed *by* the camera, which leads her to conclude that the images are pornographic, producing pleasure at the sight of suffering for the photographer and, I presume, for the consumer of these images. What emerges in the midst of this thoughtful argument is a presumption that pornography is fundamentally defined by a certain visual pleasure being taken at the sight of human and animal suffering and torture. At this point, if the pleasure is in the seeing, and is pleasure taken in the suffering depicted, then the torture is the effect

22   For a very different and provocative view that shows how the state makes use of women torturers to deflect attention from its own systemic cruelty, see Coco Fusco, *A Field Guide for Female Interrogators*, New York: Seven Stories Press, 2008.

of the camera, and the camera, or rather its pornographic gaze, is the cause of the scene of suffering itself. In effect, the camera becomes the torturer. Sometimes Bourke refers to the "perpetrators in these photographs," but at other times it seems that the photograph and the photographer are the perpetrators.[23] Both may be true in some significant sense. But the ethical problem becomes more difficult when, at the end of her provocative article, she writes that "these pornographic images have stripped bare what little force remained in the humanitarian rhetoric concerning the war."[24] I take it that she means the images give the lie to humanitarian justifications for the war. That may well be true for some, but she does not exactly say why it is true. Here it seems that the problem is not what the images depict—torture, rape, humiliation, murder—but the so-called pornography of the image itself, where pornography is defined as the pleasure taken in seeing human degradation and in the eroticization of that degradation.

This definition of pornography evacuates the photographs of the specific brutality of the scenes involved. There are examples of women torturing men, of men and women forcing Iraqi women, Muslim women, to bare their breasts, and Iraqi men, Muslim men, to perform homosexual acts or to masturbate. The torturer knows that this will cause the tortured shame; the photograph enhances the shame, provides a reflection of the act for the one who is forced into it; threatens to circulate the act as public knowledge and so as public shame. On the one hand, it appears that the US soldiers exploit the Muslim prohibition against nudity, homosexuality, and masturbation in order to tear down the cultural fabric that keeps the integrity of these people intact. On the other hand, the soldiers have their own feelings of erotic shame and fear, mixed with aggression in some very distinct ways. Why, for instance, in both the first

---

23   Bourke, "Torture as Pornography."
24   Ibid.

and second Gulf War were missiles launched against Iraq
on which American soldiers had written, "up your ass"? In
this scenario, the bombing, maiming, and killing of Iraqis is
figured through sodomy, one that is supposed to inflict the
ostensible shame of sodomy on those who are bombed. But
what does it inadvertently say about the bombers, those who
"ejaculate" the missiles? After all, it takes two to commit an
act of sodomy, which suggests that the soldiers secure their
place in the fantasized scene in the active and penetrating
position, a position that makes them no less homosexual
for being on top. That the act is figured as murder, though,
suggests that it is fully taken up in an aggressive circuit that
exploits the shame of sexuality, converting its pleasure into
a raw sadistic form. That the US prison guards continue
this fantasy by coercing their prisoners into acts of sodomy
suggests that homosexuality is equated with the decimation
of personhood, even as it is clear in these cases that it is
the torture which is responsible for that decimation.
Paradoxically, this may be a situation in which the Islamic
taboo against homosexual acts works in perfect concert
with the homophobia within the US military. The scene of
torture that includes coerced homosexual acts, and seeks to
decimate personhood through that coercion, presumes that
for both torturer and tortured, homosexuality represents the
destruction of one's being. Forcing homosexual acts would
thus seem to mean violently imposing that destruction.
The problem, of course, is that the US soldiers seek to
externalize this truth by coercing others to perform the
acts, but the witnesses, the photographers, and those who
orchestrate the scene of torture are all party to the pleasure,
exhibiting the very pleasure that they also degrade, even as
they demand to see this scene they have coercively staged
time and again. Further, the torturer, though debasing
homosexuality, can only act by becoming implicated in a
version of homosexuality in which the torturer acts as the
"top" who only penetrates and who coercively requires
that penetrability be located in the body of the tortured.

In fact, forced penetration is a mode of "assigning" that penetrability permanently elsewhere.

Obviously, Bourke is right to say that this kind of pleasure is at work in the photos and in the scenes they depict, but we make an error if we insist that the "pornography" of the photo is to blame. After all, part of what has to be explained is the excitation of the photo, the proliferation of the imagery, the relation between the acts depicted and the means through which that depiction takes place. There does seem to be a frenzy and excitement, but surely also a sexualization of the act of seeing and photographing that is distinct, though acting in tandem with, the sexualization of the scene depicted. It is not, however, the practice of eroticized seeing that is the problem here, but the moral indifference of the photograph coupled with its investment in the continuation and reiteration of the scene as a visual icon. But let us not say that the technology of the camera, digitalization, or the pornographic gaze is finally to blame for these actions. The torture may well have been incited by the presence of the camera and continued in anticipation of the camera, but this does not establish either the camera or "pornography" as its cause. Pornography, after all, has many non-violent versions and several genres that are clearly "vanilla" at best, and whose worst crime seems to be the failure to supply an innovative plot.

All of this raises an important question about the relationship between the camera and ethical responsiveness. It seems clear that these images were circulated, enjoyed, consumed, and communicated without there being any accompanying sense of moral outrage. How this particular banalization of evil took place, and why the photos failed to cause alarm, or did so only too late, or became alarming only to those outside the scenarios of war and imprisonment, are doubtless crucial to ask. One might expect that the photo would at once alert us to the abominable human suffering in the scene, and yet it has no magical moral agency of this kind. In the same way, the photograph is not the same as the torturer, even if it functions as an incitement to brutality. The photos have functioned in several ways: as an incitement to brutality within the prison itself, as a threat of shame for the prisoners, as a chronicle of a war crime, as a testimony to the radical unacceptability of torture, and as archival and documentary work made available on the internet or displayed in museums in the US, including galleries and public spaces in a host of venues.[25] The photos have clearly traveled outside the original scene, left the hands of the photographer, or turned against the photographer him or herself, even perhaps vanquished his or her pleasure. It gave rise to a different gaze than the one that would ask for a repetition of the scene, and so we probably need to accept that the photograph neither tortures nor redeems, but can be instrumentalized in radically different directions, depending on how it is discursively framed and through what form of media presentation it is displayed.

One reality we see in these photos is that of rules being ignored or broken. So the photographs function, in part, as a way of registering a certain lawlessness. What is the significance of the fact that the rules, such as they are, that were used to develop policy in Abu Ghraib were originally developed for Guantánamo? In Guantánamo, the US claimed not to be bound by the Geneva Conventions, and in Iraq it is clear that, though legally bound by those Conventions, the US defied the standards stipulated by

25   One important exhibition was Brian Wallis's "Inconvenient Evidence: Iraqi Prison Photographs from Abu Ghraib," shown simultaneously at the International Center of Photography, New York City, and The Warhol Museum, Pittsburgh (2004–5). Columbian artist Fernando Botero's paintings based on the Abu Ghraib photographs also traveled to numerous exhibitions around the US in 2006–7, most notably at the Marlborough Gallery in New York City, 2006; the Doe Library at the University of California, Berkeley, 2007; and the American University Museum, 2007. See *Botero Abu Ghraib*, Munich, Berlin, London, New York: Prestel Press, 2006, including a fine essay by David Ebony. See also the excellent work of Susan Crile, *Abu-Ghraib/Abuse of Power, Works on Paper*, exhibited at Hunter College in 2006.

them in its treatment of Iraqi prisoners. The legal move by which the US claimed that prisoners at Camp Delta were not entitled to protection under the Geneva Conventions is one that institutes the expectation that those prisoners are less than human. They are considered enemies of the state, but they are also not conceptualizable in terms of the civilizational and racial norms by which the human is constituted. In this sense, their status as less than human is not only presupposed by the torture, but reinstituted by it. And here we have to see—as Adorno cautioned us—that violence in the name of civilization reveals its own barbarism, even as it "justifies" its own violence by presuming the barbaric subhumanity of the other against whom that violence is waged.[26]

The critique of the frame is, of course, beset by the problem that the presumptive viewer is "outside" the frame, over "here" in a first-world context, and those who are depicted remain nameless and unknown. In this way, the critique I have been following stays on this side of the visual divide, offering a first-world critique of first-world visual consumption, or offering a first-world ethic and politic that would demand an outraged and informed response on the part of those whose government perpetrates or permits such torture. And the problem is clearly compounded by the fact that the publication of the most extensive set of photographs (more than 1,000) by *Salon* in February and March 2006 was constrained by international law to protect the privacy of persons who have been the victims of war crimes. It may well be that the materials received and published by *Salon* are the same as those that had been the subject of legal battles with the Department of Defense, but even if there are some images missing, the number is extensive. The files, leaked from the Criminal Investigation Command of the US army, included 1,325 images and 93 videos, though these

---

26   Theodor Adorno and Max Horkheimer, *Dialectic of Enlightenment*, trans. John Cumming, New York: Continuum, 1972; Adorno, *Minima Moralia: Reflections from Damaged Life* (1944–1947), London: Verso, 2005.

obviously do not represent the sum total of the torture. As reporter Joan Walsh pointed out in 2006, "this set of images from Abu Ghraib is only one snapshot of systematic tactics the United States has used in four-plus years of the global war on terror."[27]

Salon investigated the "captions" the US army used to identify the various scenes of torture at Abu Ghraib, and they apparently included misspellings of names and unclear accounts of time and place that had to be reconstructed. The "reality" of the events was not immediately clear on the basis of the imagery alone, and the "timeline" had to be retrospectively figured out in order to understand the evolution and systematic character of the torture itself. The question of reconstructing or, indeed, restituting the "humanity" of the victims is made all the more difficult by the fact that faces, when not already shrouded as part of the act of torture, had to be deliberately obscured to protect the privacy of the victims. What we are left with are photos of people who are for the most part faceless and nameless. But can we nevertheless say that the obscured face and the absent name function as the visual trace— even if it is a lacuna within the visible field—of the very mark of humanity? This is a mark, in other words, not registered through a norm, but by the fragments that follow in the wake of an abrogation of the normatively human. In other words, the humans who were tortured do not readily conform to a visual, corporeal, or socially recognizable identity; their occlusion and erasure become the continuing sign of their suffering and of their humanity.[28]

The point is not to substitute one set of idealized norms for understanding the "human" with another, but to grasp those instances in which the norm destroys its instance,

---

27   Joan Walsh, "Introduction: The Abu Ghraib Files," http://www.salon.com/news/abu_ghraib/2006/03/14/introduction/index.html

28   I am grateful to Eduardo Cadava for this point. See his "The Monstrosity of Human Rights" in *PMLA*, 121: 5, 2006, 1558–1565.

when human life—a human animality—exceeds and resists the norm of the human. When we speak about "humanity" in such a context, we refer to that double or trace of what is human that confounds the norm of the human or, alternatively, seeks to escape its violence. When the "human" tries to order its instances, a certain incommensurability emerges between the norm and the life it seeks to organize. Can we name that gap, and ought we to name it? Is this not the scene in which a life is apprehended that is not yet ordered by the norms of recognition?

The names of the victims are not included in the captions, but the names of the perpetrators are. Do we lament the lack of names? Yes and no. They are, and are not, ours to know. We might think that our norms of humanization require the name and the face, but perhaps the "face" works on us precisely through or as its shroud, in and through the means by which it is subsequently obscured. In this sense, the face and name are not ours to know, and affirming this cognitive limit is a way of affirming the humanity that has escaped the visual control of the photograph. To expose the victim further would be to reiterate the crime, so the task would seem to be a full documentation of the acts of the torturer, as well as a full documentation of those who exposed, disseminated, and published the scandal—but all this without intensifying the "exposure" of the victim, either through discursive or visual means.

When the photos were shown at the International Center for Photography as part of a show curated by Brian Wallis, the photographers were not credited for the pictures; the news organizations that first agreed to publish them were. Importantly, it was the publication of the photos that brought them into the public domain as objects of scrutiny. The photographer is given no credit for this; indeed the photographer, though not photographed, remains part of the scene that is published, so exposing his or her clear complicity. In this sense, the exhibition of the photographs with caption and commentary on the history of their publication and reception becomes a way of exposing and countering the closed circuit of triumphalist and sadistic exchange that formed the original scene of the photograph itself. That scene now becomes the object, and we are not so much directed by the frame as directed toward it with a renewed critical capacity.

Though we feel shock at these photographs, it is not the shock that finally informs us. In the last chapter of *Regarding the Pain of Others*, Sontag seeks to counter her earlier critique of photography. In an emotional, almost exasperated outcry, one that seems quite different from her usual measured rationalism, Sontag remarks: "Let the atrocious images haunt us."[29] Whereas earlier she diminished the power of the photograph to that of merely impressing upon us its haunting effects (whereas narrative has the power to make us understand), now it seems that some understanding is to be wrought from this very haunting. We see the photograph and cannot let go of the image that is transitively relayed to us. It brings us close to an understanding of the fragility and mortality of human life, the stakes of death in the scene of politics. She seemed to know this already in *On Photography* when she wrote: "Photographs state the innocence, the vulnerability of lives heading toward their own destruction, and this link between photography and death haunts all photographs of people."[30]

Perhaps Sontag is influenced by Roland Barthes at such a moment, since it was Barthes, in *Camera Lucida*, who argued that the photographic image has a particular capacity to cast a face, a life, in the tense of the future anterior.[31]

29　Sontag, *Regarding the Pain of Others*, 65.

30　Sontag, *On Photography*, 70.

31　Barthes, *Camera Lucida: Reflections on Photography*. I am indebted to John Muse's excellent dissertation in the Department of Rhetoric, "The Rhetorical Afterlife of Photographic Evidence" (University of California, Berkeley, 2007), for inspiring some of these reflections, and to Amy Huber for reminding me of Barthes' comments here and for the challenge of her dissertation "The General Theatre of Death: Modern Fatality and Modernist Form" (University of California, Berkeley, 2009).

The photograph relays less the present moment than the perspective, the pathos, of a time in which "this will have been." The photograph operates as a visual chronicle: it "does not necessarily say *what is no longer*, but only and for certain *what has been*."[32] But every photographic portrait speaks in at least two temporal modes, both a chronicle of what has been and protentive certainty about what will have been. Barthes writes famously of what the photograph bespeaks of Lewis Payne in jail waiting to be hanged: "*he is going to die*. I read at the same time: *This will be* and *this has been*. I observe with horror an anterior future of which death is the stake *(dont le mort est l'enjeu)*. By giving me the absolute past of the pose (aorist), the photograph tells me death in the future."[33] But this quality is not reserved for those overtly condemned to death by courts of law, or indeed for those already dead, since for Barthes "every photograph is this catastrophe," installing and soliciting a perspective on the absolute pastness of a life.[34]

Under what conditions does this quality of "absolute pastness" counter the forces of melancholy and open up a more explicit form of grieving? Is this quality of "absolute pastness" that is conferred on a living being, one whose life is not past, precisely the quality of grievability? To confirm that a life was, even within the life itself, is to underscore that a life is a grievable life. In this sense the photograph, through its relation to the future anterior, instates grievability. It makes sense to wonder whether this insight is not related to Sontag's imperative: "Let the atrocious images haunt us."[35] Her imperative suggests that there are conditions in which we can refuse to be haunted, or where haunting cannot reach us. If we are not haunted, there is no loss, there has been no life that was lost. But if we are shaken or

32 Barthes, *Camera Lucida*, 85.
33 Ibid., 96.
34 Ibid.
35 Sontag, *Regarding the Pain of Others*, 115.

"haunted" by a photograph, it is because the photograph acts on us in part through outliving the life it documents; it establishes in advance the time in which that loss will be acknowledged as a loss. So the photograph is linked through its "tense" to the grievability of a life, anticipating and performing that grievability. In this way, we can be haunted in advance by the suffering or deaths of others. Or we can be haunted afterwards, when the check against grief becomes undone. It is not only or exclusively at an affective register that the photograph operates, but through instituting a certain mode of acknowledgment. It "argues" for the grievability of a life: its pathos is at once affective and interpretive. If we can be haunted, then we can acknowledge that there has been a loss and hence that there has been a life: this is an initial moment of cognition, an apprehension, but also a potential judgment, and it requires that we conceive of grievability as the precondition of life, one that is discovered retrospectively through the temporality instituted by the photograph itself. "Someone will have lived" is spoken within a present, but it refers to a time and a loss to come. Thus the anticipation of the past underwrites the photograph's distinctive capacity to establish grievability as a precondition of a knowable human life—to be haunted is precisely to apprehend that life before precisely knowing it.

Sontag herself makes less ambitious claims. She writes that the photograph can be an "invitation ... to pay attention, reflect ... examine the rationalizations for mass suffering offered by established powers."[36] It is my sense that the curated exhibition of the Abu Ghraib photos at the International Center for Photography did precisely that. But what is most interesting to me about the increasing outrage and exasperation Sontag expressed in her writings on 9/11 and in her article "Regarding the Torture of Others" is that it continued to be directed against the photograph

36   Ibid., 117.

not only for making her feel outrage, but for failing to show her how to transform that affect into effective political action. She acknowledges that she has in the past turned against the photograph with moralistic denunciation precisely because it enrages without directing the rage, and so excites our moral sentiments at the same time as it confirms our political paralysis. And even this frustration frustrates her, since it seems a guilty and narcissistic preoccupation with what one can do as a first-world intellectual, and so fails again to attend to the suffering of others. Even at the end of that consideration, it is a museum piece by Jeff Wall that allows Sontag to formulate this problem of responding to the pain of others, and so, we might surmise, involves a certain consolidation of the museum world as the one within which she is most likely to find room for reflection and deliberation. At this moment, we can see her turn both from the photograph and from the political exigencies of war to the museum exhibition that gives her the time and space for the kind of thinking and writing she treasures. She confirms her position as an intellectual, but shows us how this piece might help us to reflect more carefully about war. In this context, Sontag asks whether the tortured can and do look back, and what they see when they look at us. She was faulted for saying that the photographs from Abu Ghraib were photographs of "us," and some critics suggested that this was again a kind of self-preoccupation that paradoxically and painfully took the place of a reflection on the suffering of others. But what she asked was "whether the nature of the policies prosecuted by this administration and the hierarchies deployed to carry them out makes such acts [of torture] likely. Considered in this light, the photographs are us."[37]

Perhaps she was saying that in seeing the photos, we see ourselves seeing, that we are those photographers to the extent that we share the norms that provide the frames in

37   Sontag, "Regarding the Torture of others."

which those lives are rendered destitute and abject, and are sometimes clearly beaten to death. In Sontag's view, the dead are profoundly uninterested in us—they do not seek our gaze. This rebuff to visual consumerism that comes from the shrouded head, the averted glance, the glazed eyes, this indifference to us performs an auto-critique of the role of the photograph within media consumption. Although we might want to see, the photograph tells us clearly that the dead do not care whether we see or not. For Sontag, this is the ethical force of the photograph, to mirror back the final narcissism of our desire to see and to refuse satisfaction to that narcissistic demand.

She may be right, but perhaps it is also our inability to see what we see that is also of critical concern. To learn to see the frame that blinds us to what we see is no easy matter. And if there is a critical role for visual culture during times of war it is precisely to thematize the forcible frame, the one that conducts the dehumanizing norm, that restricts what is perceivable and, indeed, what can be. Although restriction is necessary for focus, and there is no seeing without selection, this restriction we have been asked to live with imposes constraints on what can be heard, read, seen, felt, and known, and so works to undermine both a sensate understanding of war, and the conditions for a sensate opposition to war. This "not seeing" in the midst of seeing, this not seeing that is the condition of seeing, became the visual norm, a norm that has been a national norm, one conducted by the photographic frame in the scene of torture. In this case, the circulation of the image outside the scene of its production has broken up the mechanism of disavowal, scattering grief and outrage in its wake.

3

Sexual Politics, Torture, and Secular Time

To say that one would like to consider sexual politics during this time raises an immediate problem, since it seems clear that one cannot reference "this time" without knowing which time is being referred to, where that time takes hold, and for whom a certain consensus might emerge on the issue of what time this is. If the problem is not just a matter of different interpretations of what time it is, then it would seem that we already have more than one time at work in this time, and that the problem of time will afflict any effort I might make to try to consider such issues now. It might seem odd to begin with a reflection on time when one is trying to speak about sexual politics and cultural politics more broadly. But I want to suggest that the way in which debates within sexual politics are framed is already imbued with the problem of time, and of progress in particular, and with certain notions of what it means to unfold a future of freedom in time. That there is no one time, that the question of what time this is, already divides us, has to do with which histories have turned out to be formative, how they intersect—or fail to intersect—with other histories, and so with a question of how temporality is organized along spatial lines.

I am not suggesting here that we return to a version of cultural difference that depends on cultural wholism, i.e.

that cultures ought to be regarded as discrete and self-identical unities, monolithic and distinct. In fact, I oppose any such return. The problem is not that there are different cultures at war with one another, or that there are different modalities of time, each conceived as self-sufficient, that are articulated in different and differentiated cultural locations or that come into confused or brutal contact with one another. Of course, that could be, at some level, a valid description, but it would miss an important point, namely, that hegemonic conceptions of progress define themselves over and against a pre-modern temporality that they produce for the purposes of their own self-legitimation. Politically, the questions—"What time are we in?" "Are all of us in the same time?" and specifically, "Who has arrived in modernity and who has not?"—are all raised in the midst of very serious political contestations. The questions cannot be answered through recourse to a simple culturalism.

It is my view that sexual politics, rather than operating at the margin of this contestation, is in the middle of it, and that very often claims to new or radical sexual freedoms are appropriated precisely by that point of view—usually enunciated from within state power—that would try to define Europe and the sphere of modernity as the privileged site where sexual radicalism can and does take place. Often, but not always, the further claim is made that such a privileged site of radical freedom must be protected against the putative orthodoxies associated with new immigrant communities. I will let that claim stand for the moment, since it carries with it a host of presuppositions that will be considered later in this chapter. But we should remember from the outset that this is a suspect formulation, one regularly made by a state discourse that seeks to produce distinct notions of sexual minorities and of new immigrant communities within a temporal trajectory that would make Europe and its state apparatus into the avatar of both freedom and modernity.

In my view, the problem is not that there are different temporalities in different cultural locations—so that, accordingly, we simply need to broaden our cultural frameworks to become more internally complicated and capacious. That form of pluralism accepts the distinct and wholistic framing for each of these so-called "communities" and then poses an artificial question about how the tensions between them might be overcome. The problem, rather, is that certain notions of relevant geopolitical space—including the spatial boundedness of minority communities—are circumscribed by this story of a progressive modernity; certain notions of what "this time" can and must be are similarly construed on the basis of circumscribing the "where" of its happening. I should make clear that I am not opposing all notions of "moving forward" and am certainly not against all versions of "progress," but I am profoundly influenced, if not dislocated, by Walter Benjamin's graphic rethinking of progress and the time of the "now," and that is part of what I am bringing to bear on a consideration of sexual politics. I want to say: a consideration of sexual politics *now*, and of course that is the case, but perhaps my thesis is simply that there can be no consideration of sexual politics without a critical consideration of the time of the now. My claim will be that thinking through the problem of temporality and politics in this way may open up a different approach to cultural difference, one that eludes the claims of pluralism and intersectionality alike.

The point is not just to become mindful of the temporal and spatial presuppositions of some of our progressive narratives, the ones that inform various parochial, if not structurally racist, political optimisms of various kinds. The point is rather to show that our understanding of what is happening "now" is bound up with a certain geopolitical restriction on imagining the relevant borders of the world and even a refusal to understand what happens to our notion of time if we take the problem of the border (what crosses the border and what does not, and the means and mechanisms of that crossing or impasse) to be central to any understanding of contemporary political life. The contemporary map of sexual politics is crossed, I would say, with contentions and antagonisms that define the time of sexual politics as a fractious constellation. The story of progress is but one strand within that constellation, and one that has, for good reason, come into crisis.[1]

My interest lies in focusing on how certain secular conceptions of history and of what is meant by a "progressive" position within contemporary politics rely on a conception of freedom that is understood to emerge through time, and which is temporally progressive in its structure.[2] This link between freedom and temporal progress is often what is being indexed when pundits and public policy representatives refer to concepts like modernity or, indeed, secularism. I don't want to suggest that this is all they mean, but I do want to say that a certain conception of freedom is invoked precisely as a rationale and instrument for certain practices of coercion, and this places those of us who have conventionally understood ourselves as advocating a progressive sexual politics in a rather serious bind.

In this context, I want to point to a few sites of political debate involving both sexual politics and anti-Islamic practice which suggest that certain ideas concerning the progress of "freedom" facilitate a political division between progressive sexual politics and the struggles against racism and religious discrimination. One of the issues that follows from such a re-constellation is that a certain version and deployment of the notion of "freedom" can be used as an instrument of bigotry

---

1 See Wendy Brown, *Politics Out Of History*, Princeton, NJ: Princeton University Press, 2001.

2 Janet Jakobsen and Ann Pellegrini, *Love the Sin: Sexual Regulation and the Limits of Religious Tolerance*, New York: New York University Press, 2004; Saba Mahmood, *The Politics of Piety*, Princeton, NJ: Princeton University Press, 2005; Talal Asad, *Formations of the Secular: Christianity, Islam, Modernity*, Palo Alto: Stanford University Press, 2003; and William E. Connolly, *Why I Am Not a Secularist*, Minneapolis: University of Minnesota Press, 2000.

and coercion. This happens most frightfully when women's sexual freedom or the freedom of expression and association for lesbian and gay people is invoked instrumentally to wage a cultural assault on Islam that reaffirms US sovereignty and violence. Must we rethink freedom and its implication in the narrative of progress, or must we seek to resituate freedom outside of those narrative constraints? My point is surely not to abandon freedom as a norm, but to ask about its uses, and to consider how it must be rethought if we are to resist its coercive instrumentalization in the present and if it is to take on another meaning that might remain useful for a radical democratic politics.

In the Netherlands, for instance, new applicants for immigration are asked to look at photos of two men kissing and to report on whether the photos are offensive, whether they are understood to express personal liberties, and whether the viewers are willing to live in a democracy that values the rights of gay people to free expression.[3] Those who are in favor of this policy claim that acceptance of homosexuality is the same as acceptance of modernity. We can see in such an instance how modernity is being defined as linked to sexual freedom, and the sexual freedom of gay people in particular is understood to exemplify a culturally advanced position, as opposed to one that would be deemed pre-modern. It would seem that the Dutch government has made special arrangements for a class of people who are considered presumptively modern. The presumptively modern includes the following groups who are exempt from having to take the test: European Union nationals, asylum-seekers and skilled workers who earn more than

---

3   As reported in http://www.msnbc.msn.com/id/11842116. The statement can be found on the website of the Dutch Immigration and Naturalization Service (IND), at http://www.ind.nl/en/inbedrijf/actueel/basisexamen_inburgering.asp. Note that more recent revisions to this policy now offer two versions of the exam so that the visual images of nudity and homosexuality are not obligatory viewing by religious minorities whose faith might be offended. The matter continues to be contested in Dutch and European courts.

€45,000 per year, and citizens of the US, Australia, New Zealand, Canada, Japan, and Switzerland—where either homophobia is not to be found, or else the importing of impressive income levels has here taken precedence over the dangers of importing homophobia.[4]

In the Netherlands, of course, this movement has been brewing for some time. The identification of gay politics with cultural and political modernity was emblematized within European politics in the figure of Pim Fortuyn, the gay and overtly anti-Islamic politician who was gunned down by a radical environmentalist in the winter of 2002. A similar conflict was also dramatized in the work and the death of Theo van Gogh, who came to stand not for sexual freedom but for principles of political and artistic freedom. Of course, I am in favor of such freedoms, but it seems that I must now also ask whether these freedoms for which I have struggled, and continue to struggle, are being instrumentalized in order to establish a specific cultural grounding, secular in a particular sense, that functions as a prerequisite for admission of the acceptable immigrant. In what follows, I will elaborate further what this cultural grounding is, how it functions as both transcendental condition and teleological aim, and how it complicates any simple distinctions we might make between the secular and the religious.

In the present instance, a set of cultural norms is being articulated that are considered preconditions of citizenship. We might accept the view that there always are such norms, and even that full civic and cultural participation for anyone, regardless of gender or sexual orientation, requires such norms. But the question is whether they are articulated not only differentially, but also instrumentally,

---

4   Note that changes were made in the Dutch Civic Integration Exam in 2008 in order to show greater cultural sensitivity to new immigrant communities. In July 2008 the exam was ruled illegal in its current form. See htttp://www.minbuza. nl/en/welcome/comingtoNL,visas_x_consular_services/civic_integration_ examination_abroad.html, and http://www.hrw.org/en/news/2008/07/16/nether-lands-court-rules-pre-entry-integration-exam-unlawful

in order to shore up particular religious and cultural preconditions that affect other sorts of exclusions. One is not free to reject this cultural grounding since it is the basis, even the presumptive prerequisite, of the operative notion of freedom, and freedom is articulated through a set of graphic images, figures that come to stand for what freedom can and must be. And so a certain paradox ensues in which the coerced adoption of certain cultural norms becomes a prerequisite for entry into a polity that defines itself as the avatar of freedom. Is the Dutch government engaging in civic pedagogy through its defense of lesbian and gay sexual freedom, and would it impose its test on right-wing white supremacists, such as Vlaams Blok (now Vlaams Belang), who are congregated on its border with Belgium and who have called for a *cordon sanitaire* around Europe to keep out the non-Europeans? Is it administering tests to lesbian and gay people to make sure they are not offended by the visible practices of Muslim minorities? If the civic integration exam were part of a wider effort to foster cultural understanding about religious and sexual norms for a diverse Dutch population, one that included new pedagogies and funding for public arts projects dedicated to this purpose, we might then understand cultural "integration" in a different sense; but we certainly cannot do so if it is coercively administered. In this case, though, the question raised is this: Is the exam a means for testing tolerance, or does it in fact represent an assault against religious minorities that is part of a broader coercive effort on the part of the state to demand that they rid themselves of their traditional religious beliefs and practices in order to gain entry into the Netherlands? Is the test a liberal defense of my freedom with which I should be pleased, or is my freedom here being used as an instrument of coercion—one that seeks to keep Europe white, pure, and "secular" in ways that do not interrogate the violence that underwrites that very project? Certainly, I want to be able to kiss in public—don't get me wrong.

But do I want to insist that everyone must watch and approve of kissing in public before they can acquire rights of citizenship? I think not.

If the prerequisites of the polity require either cultural homogeneity or a model of cultural pluralism, then, either way, the solution is figured as assimilation to a set of cultural norms that are understood as internally self-sufficient and self-standing. These norms are not in conflict, open to dispute, in contact with other norms, contested or disrupted in a field in which a number of norms converge—or fail to converge—in an ongoing way. The presumption is that culture is a uniform and binding groundwork of norms, and not an open field of contestation, temporally dynamic; this groundwork only functions if it is uniform or integrated, and that desideratum is required, even forcibly, for something called modernity to emerge and take hold. Of course, we can already see that this very specific sense of modernity entails an immunization against contestation, that it is maintained through a dogmatic grounding, and that already we are introduced to a kind of dogmatism that belongs to a particular secular formation. Within this framework the freedom of personal expression, broadly construed, relies upon the suppression of a mobile and contested understanding of cultural difference, and the issue makes clear how state violence invests in cultural homogeneity as it applies its exclusionary policies to rationalize state policies towards Islamic immigrants.[5]

I do not traffic in theories of modernity because the concept of modernity strikes me as too general. Such theories are, in my view, for the most part too broad and sketchy to be useful, and people from different disciplines mean very different things by them. I merely note here the way such theories function in these arguments, and

---

5   See Marc de Leeuw and Sonja van Wichelin, "'Please, Go Wake Up!' Submission, Hirsi Ali, and the 'War on Terror' in The Netherlands," *Feminist Media Studies* 5: 3 (2005).

restrict my comments to those kinds of uses. It makes sense to trace the discursive uses of modernity—which is something other than supplying a theory. In this regard, the concept seems to function neither as a signifier of cultural multiplicity nor of normative schemes that are dynamically or critically in flux, and certainly not as a model of cultural contact, translation, convergence, or divergence.

To the extent that both artistic expression and sexual freedom are understood as ultimate signs of this developmental version of modernity, and are conceived as rights supported by a particular formation of secularism, we are asked to disarticulate struggles for sexual freedom from struggles against racism and anti-Islamic sentiment and conduct. There is presumably no solidarity among such efforts within a framework such as the one I have just outlined, though we could of course point to existing coalitions that defy this logic. Indeed, according to this view, struggles for sexual expression depend upon the restriction and foreclosure of rights of religious expression (if we are to stay within the liberal framework), producing an antinomy within the discourse of liberal rights itself. But it seems to me that something more fundamental is occurring, namely, that liberal freedoms are now being understood to rely upon a hegemonic culture, one that is called "modernity" and that relies on a certain progressive account of increasing freedoms. This uncritical domain of "culture" functioning as a precondition for liberal freedom in turn becomes the cultural basis for sanctioning forms of cultural and religious hatred and abjection.

My point is not to trade sexual freedoms for religious ones, but, rather, to question the framework that assumes there can be no political analysis that tries to analyze homophobia and racism in ways that move beyond this antinomy of liberalism. At stake is whether or not there can be a convergence or alliance between such struggles or whether the struggle against homophobia must contradict the struggle against cultural and religious racisms. If that framework of mutual exclusion holds—one that is derived,

I would suggest, from a restrictive idea of personal liberty bound up with a restrictive conception of progress—then it would appear that there are no points of cultural contact between sexual progressives and religious minorities other than encounters of violence and exclusion. But if, in place of a liberal conception of personal freedom, we focus on the critique of state violence and the elaboration of its coercive mechanisms, we may well arrive at an alternative political framework, one that implies another sense not only of modernity, but also of the time, the "now," in which we live.

It was Thomas Friedman who claimed in the *New York Times* that Islam has not yet achieved modernity, suggesting that it is somehow in a childish state of cultural development and that the norm of adulthood is represented more adequately by critics such as himself.[6] In this sense, then, Islam is conceived as not of *this* time or *our* time, but of *another* time, one that has only anachronistically emerged in this time. But is not such a view precisely the refusal to think of this time not as one time, or as one story, developing unilinearly, but as a convergence of histories that have not always been thought together, and whose convergence or lack thereof presents a set of quandaries that might be said to be definitive of our time?

A similar dynamic is to be found in France, where questions of sexual politics converge in some unhappy ways with anti-immigration politics. Of course, there are profound differences as well. In contemporary France, the culture publicly defended against new immigrant communities draws only selectively on normative ideals that structure debates on sexual politics. For instance, dominant French opinion draws upon rights of contract that have been extended through new sexual politics at the same time as it limits those very rights of contract when they threaten

6   Thomas Friedman, "Foreign Affairs: The Real War," *New York Times*, November 27, 2001, A19.

to disrupt patrilineal kinship and its links to masculinist norms of nationhood. Ideas of "culture" and of "*laïcité*" (or secularism) work differently, and one sees how a certain kind of ostensibly progressive sexual politics is again sanctioned as the logical culmination of a secular realization of freedom at the same time as that very same conception of secular freedom operates as a norm to exclude or minimize the possibility of ethnic and religious communities from North Africa, Turkey, and the Middle East from attaining full rights of civic and legal membership. Indeed, the situation is even more complex than this analysis would suggest, since the idea of culture, bound up with a conception of symbolic law, is regarded as founding the freedom to enter into free associations, but is also invoked to limit the freedom of lesbian and gay people to adopt children or gain access to reproductive technology, thus avowing the rights of contract but refusing challenges to the norms of kinship. The arguments that secured legislative victory for PACS (*pacte civil de solidarité*)—those legal partnerships into which any two people, regardless of gender, may enter—are based on an extension of those rights to form contracts on the basis of one's own volition.[7] And yet, once the cultural preconditions of that freedom are abrogated, the law intervenes to maintain—or even mandate—that cultural integrity.

One can rather quickly conclude, for instance, on the basis of a variety of opinions published in French journals and newspapers, that there exists a widely held belief that gay and lesbian parenting runs the risk of producing a psychotic child. The extraordinary support among French republicans for PACS has depended from the start on its separation from any rights to adoption or to parenting structures outside the heterosexual norm. In the newspapers and throughout public discourse, social

---

7   D. Borillo, E. Fassin, and M. Iacub, *Au-delà du PACS*, Paris: Presses Universitaires de France, 2004.

psychologists argue that lesbian or gay parenting—and this would include single-mother parenting as well—threatens to undermine the very framework that a child requires in order (a) to know and understand sexual difference, and (b) to gain an orientation in the cultural world. The presumption is that if a child has no father, that child will not come to understand masculinity in the culture, and, if it is a boy child, he will have no way to embody or incorporate his own masculinity. This argument assumes many things, but chief among them is the idea that the institution of fatherhood is the sole or major cultural instrument for the reproduction of masculinity. Even if we were to accept the problematic normative claim that a boy child ought to be reproducing masculinity (and there are very good reasons to question this assumption), any child has access to a range of masculinities that are embodied and transmitted through a variety of cultural means. The "adult world," as Jean Laplanche puts it in an effort to formulate a psychoanalytic alternative to the Oedipal triad, impresses its cultural markers on the child from any number of directions, and the child, whether boy or girl, must fathom and reckon with those norms. But in France the notion of a "framework of orientation"—called *"le repère"*—is understood to be uniquely transmitted by the father. And this symbolic function is ostensibly threatened or even destroyed by having two fathers, or an intermittent father, or no father at all. One has to struggle not to get lured into this fight on these terms, since the fight misconstrues the issue at stake. If one were to get lured into it, one could, of course, make the rejoinder that masculinity can certainly be embodied and communicated by a parent of another gender. However, if I argue that way, I concede the premise that the parent is and must be the unique cultural site for the communication and reproduction of gender, and that would be a foolish point to concede. After all, why accept the idea that without a single embodied referent for masculinity, there can be no cultural orientation as such? Such a position makes the singular masculinity of the father into the transcendental condition of culture rather than rethinking masculinity and fatherhood as a set of disarticulated, variable, and variably significant cultural practices. To understand this debate, it is important to remember that lines of patrilineality in France are secured in the civil code through rights of filiation. To the extent that heterosexual marriage maintains its monopoly on reproduction, it does so precisely through privileging the biological father as the representative of national culture.[8]

Thus the debates on sexual politics invariably become bound up with the politics of new immigrant communities, since both rely on foundational ideas of culture that precondition the allocation of basic legal entitlements. If we understand these ideas of culture as secular, then it seems to me that we may well not have a sufficient vocabulary for understanding the traditions from which these ideas of culture are formed—and by which they continue to be informed—or the force by which they are maintained. Here it becomes clear that the theories of psychological development that produce the patrilineal conditions of national culture constitute the "norms of adulthood" that precondition the substantive rights of citizenship. In this way, Ségolène Royal, the 2006 French Socialist Party presidential nominee, could join the successful candidate Nicolas Sarkozy in arguing that les émeutes, the 2005 riots, in the banlieues were the direct consequence of a deterioration in family structures represented by new immigrant communities.[9] The theme of a certain childishness re-emerges in this context as well, such that we are invited to understand the political expressions

8   See Eric Fassin, *L'inversion de la question homosexuelle*, Paris: Éditions Amsterdam, 2006; and Didier Fassin and E. Fassin, *De la question sociale à la question raciale?* Paris: La Decouverte, 2006.

9   *Libération*, June 2, 2006, http://www.liberation.fr/actualite/evenement/evenement1/371.FR.php

of Islamic minorities as failures of psycho-cultural development. These kinds of arguments parallel the parent/child relation that Thomas Friedman articulated in relation to secular modernity, where the "parent" figured as a fully developed adult. Anachronistic Islam is figured here as the child who suffers permanently from thwarted development. Family politics, even the heterosexual ordering of the family, functions to secure the temporal sequence that establishes French culture at the forefront of modernity. This version of modernity involves an odd situation in which an intractable developmental law sets limits on volitional freedom, but the contract form extends freedom almost limitlessly. In other words, contracts can be extended to any pair of consenting adults—the legal achievement of PACS has become relatively normalized for both straight and lesbian/gay couples. But such partnerships have to be rigorously separated from kinship that, by definition, precedes and limits the contract form. These norms of kinship are referenced by the term *l'ordre symbolique*, the symbolic order, which actually functions in public discourse, and it is this order that has to be protected, underwriting contract relations just as it must be immunized against a full saturation by those relations. Whether or not such an order is unambiguously secular is, in my view, another question, an open question, but there are many reasons to ask how far it transmits and maintains certain predominantly Catholic theological notions. This becomes explicitly clear, for instance, in the work of anthropologist Françoise Héritier, who argues, on Catholic grounds, that the symbolic order is both theologically derived and a prerequisite of psycho-social development.

The refusal to grant legal recognition for gay parenting works in tandem with anti-Islamic state policies to support a cultural order that keeps heterosexual normativity tied to a racist conception of culture. Conceived as pervasively paternal and nationalist, this order is equally, if differently, threatened by those kinship arrangements understood to be operative in new immigrant communities that fail to uphold the patriarchal and marital basis of the family, which in turn produces the intelligible parameters of culture and the possibility of a "knowing orientation" within that culture. Of course, what is most peculiar about this critique of the absent father in the *banlieues* is not only that it can be found among both socialists and their right-wing foes, but that it fails to recognize that contemporary immigration law is itself partially responsible for re-forging kinship ties in certain ways. After all, the French government has been willing to separate children from parents, to keep families from reunifying, and to maintain inadequate social services for new immigrant communities. Indeed, some critics have gone so far as to argue that social services constitute the emasculation of the state itself.

Such views are articulated by Michel Schneider, a psychoanalyst who in offering his opinions on cultural affairs has publicly maintained that the state must step in to take the place of the absent father, not through welfare benefits (itself conceived as a maternal deformation of the state), but through the imposition of law, discipline, and uncompromising modes of punishment and imprisonment.[10] In his view, this is the only way to secure the cultural foundations of citizenship, that is, the cultural foundations that are required for the exercise of a certain conception of freedom. Thus, the state policies that create extreme class differentials, pervasive racism in employment practices, efforts to separate families in order to save children from Islamic formations, and efforts to sequester the *banlieues* as intensified sites of racialized poverty, are exonerated and effaced through such explanations. Anti-racist demonstrations such as those that took place in 2005 took aim at property, not persons, and yet they

---

10   Michael Schneider, *Big Mother: Psychopathologie de la vie politique*, Paris: Odile Jacob, 2005.

were widely interpreted as the violent and a-relational acts of young men whose family structures were lacking firm paternal authority.[11] A certain prohibitive "no," it is argued, was absent from the family and the culture, and the state must therefore act as a compensatory paternal authority in such a situation. That the state then develops a host of reasons for regulating family and school in the *banlieue* is further proof that the state responds to such insurgency through consolidating and augmenting its power in relation to biopolitics and kinship arrangements at every level. We might conclude, therefore, that at a basic level, the entitlement to a notion of freedom based on contract is limited by those freedoms that might extend the contract too far, that is, to the point of disrupting the cultural preconditions of contractarianism itself. In other words, disruptions in family formation or in kinship arrangements that do not support the lines of patrilineality and the corollary norms of citizenship rationalize state prohibitions and regulations that augment state power in the image of the father, that missing adult, that cultural fetish which signifies a maturity based upon violence.

The rules that define culture as supported by the heterosexual family are clearly also those that set the prerequisites for entering into citizenship. Although in France these rules form the basis of *laïcité* and supply the grounds for state intervention to protect the rights of men against cultural incursions from without, they function in an analogous way to the papal arguments that condemn gay parenting and Islamic religious practice on common theological grounds. In both cases, there are culturally specific rules or laws that set a limit to contractual relations in the sphere of family and kinship and, indeed, to the field of recognizability. This parallelism raises the question of the status of this idea of culture as part of

---

11   See Nacira Guénif-Souilamas, *La république mise à nu par son immigration*, Paris: La Fabrique Éditions, 2006.

secular modernity and, in particular, whether the symbolic order is finally a secular concept (and if so, what this tells us about the impurity of secularism). In particular, it raises the question of whether the symbolic order, understood as a binding and uniform set of rules that constitute culture, functions in alliance with theological norms governing kinship. This view, interestingly enough, is not far from the Pope's conviction that the heterosexual family is what secures gender in its natural place, a natural place that inscribes a divine order.[12] Whereas in France the notion of "culture" is precisely what communicates the universal necessity of sexual difference, understood as the

---

12   Ratzinger goes on to make clear how the doctrine of sexual difference he defends is rooted in the story of Genesis, a story that establishes the "truth" of men and women. His opposition to gay marriage, which seeks to "destroy" that truth, is thus linked with his implicit creationism. One could simply reply by saying, yes, the truth of man and woman that you outline is no truth at all and we seek to destroy it in order to give rise to a more humane and radical set of gender practices. But to speak this way is simply to reiterate the cultural divide that makes no analysis possible. Perhaps one needs to start with the status of the story of Genesis itself and to see what other readings are possible. Perhaps one needs to ask which biology Ratzinger actually accepts, and whether the biological theories he supports are ones that consider homosexuality to be a benign aspect of human sexual variation. It seems that his remark about social constructionists seeking to deny and transcend biological differences commits him to a theological reading of social construction, since that "transcendence" is, presumably, what is to be sought for in the "sacralization" of sexuality in terms of its transcendent function. Can it be shown that the biological differences to which Ratzinger refers are actually consonant with the transcendent meanings he reserves for heterosexual sexuality in the service of reproduction? In addition to finding out which biological account Ratzinger has in mind, it would be important to understand whether the social practices he seeks to curb, including civil unions for same-sex partners, are either prescribed or proscribed by any ostensible biological function. The point is not to deny biology and embrace a voluntaristic self-making, but to ask how biology and social practice are understood in relation to one another. More recently, the Pope has suggested that the theory that gender is socially constructed is analogous to the destruction of the rainforest, since both seek to deny creationism. See "Meditation on Gender Lands Pope in Hot Water," *Independent*, December 23, 2008; as well as a feminist reply by Angela McRobbie, "The Pope Doth Protest Too Much," *Guardian*, January 18, 2009.

unequivocal difference between masculine and feminine, in present-day Catholic theology, we find that the family not only requires two discrete sexes, but is obligated to embody and reproduce sexual difference as both a cultural and theological necessity.

In 2004, before becoming Pope, Ratzinger considered two approaches to women's issues in his "Letter to the Bishops of the Catholic Church on the Collaboration of Men and Women in the Church and the World."[13] The first, he maintains, sustains an oppositional relationship to men. The second seems to pertain to the new gender politics that takes gender to be a variable social function. Ratzinger characterizes this second strand of feminism with the following language:

> In order to avoid the domination of one sex or the other, their differences tend to be denied, viewed as mere effects of historical and cultural conditioning. In this perspective, physical difference, termed sex, is minimized, while the purely cultural element, termed gender, is emphasized to the maximum and held to be primary. The obscuring of the difference or duality of the sexes has enormous consequences on a variety of levels. This theory of the human person, intended to promote prospects for equality of women through liberation from biological determinism, has in reality inspired ideologies which, for example, call into question the family, in its natural two-parent structure of mother and father, and make homosexuality and heterosexuality virtually equivalent, in a new model of polymorphous sexuality.[14]

He goes further, suggesting that this second approach to women's issues is rooted in a motivation understood as:

---

13   http://www.vatican.va/roman_curia/congregations/cfaith/documents/rc_con_cfaith_doc_20040731_collaboration_en.html
14   Ibid.

the human attempt to be freed from one's biological conditioning. According to this perspective, human nature in itself does not possess characteristics in an absolute manner: all persons can and ought to constitute themselves as they like, since they are free from every predetermination linked to their essential constitution.[15]

In France, the view that culture itself is carried by the heterosexual family, patrilineally defined, is communicated clearly through the notion that a child without heterosexual parentage will not only be without cognitive orientation, but will be precluded from the cultural and cognitive prerequisites of citizenship. This explains in part why France was able to extend rights of contract through the passage of the PACS while opposing every effort to legalize gay parenting. It is linked to the conviction that new immigrant communities lack a strong paternal figure, and that full rights of citizenship require subjection to an embodiment of paternal law. For some French politicians, this analysis leads to the conclusion that the state must enter into the regulation of the family where it is perceived that strong fathers do not exist. This has actually led to the forced separation of parents and children through new immigration policy, i.e., one that works in favor of the father and so of the symbolic family, even if it means destroying existing ones.

If the Pope refers to the natural laws of culture when he opposes gay and lesbian sexuality and non-heterosexual parenting arrangements, he refers to civilization when he makes his indirect denunciations of Islam. In late 2006, of course, the Pope publicly cited a document that

---

15   I would prefer to position myself in neither way, but what way is then left? Ratzinger characterizes positions here without citation, so while it appears he may have read sources for some of them, he is not beholden to any textual evidence in making his claims. Scripture, of course, is cited, but the positions that defy or threaten scripture are clearly not (as far as my research has yielded).

contained the following denunciation of Islam: "Show me just what Mohammed brought that was new, and there you will find things only evil and inhuman, such as his command to spread by the sword the faith he preached."[16] Ratzinger claimed that this statement was not his, that he was only citing it, but if one looks closely at his speech it becomes clear that he cites it, distances himself from it, and then mobilizes it to issue a warning about the current threat to civilization that Islam represents. Of course, there are many ways to approach this rather astonishing declaration, most obviously by pointing to the bloodshed through which Christianity sought to spread its own faith over many centuries. But I'd like briefly to point to the word "inhuman," since it is coupled with "evil" and we have already considered what the Pope thinks about the cultural foundations of the human as such.

Additionally, as the sword is prohibited as a means of coercing faith in the Qur'an, it surely becomes a term of transference in this scenario, since to whom did the sword belong when it operated in the service of forced conversion if not to Christianity? Precisely because swords are not the weapons of choice in a contemporary sense, they evince a mythical time, a tribalist archaism, and also become precisely the nexus of fantasy. I could go on at length, but I want here only to point out the extraordinary inversion of history that the word "sword" permits, and the enormous ideological force of distinguishing between the human, as that which is presumably only supported by a Judeo-Christian culture, and the "inhuman" and "evil" as what follows from a departure from that culture. Let's remember, as Uri Avnery points out, that Islam was never forced upon the Jews, that when Spain was conquered by

16   "Faith, Reason and the University: Memories and Reflections," a speech given at the University of Regensburg, September 12, 2006. The speech and subsequent explanations can be found at http://www.vatican.va/holy_father/ benedict_xvi/speeches/2006/september/documents/hf_ben-xvi_spe_20060912_ university-regensburg_en.html

Catholics and the Muslims were dispossessed of power, the Inquisition was turned against both Muslims and Jews, and that Sephardic Jews found hospitality in Arab countries for fifty generations.[17]

When the Pope refers to this "sword" wielded by those who are less than human, we have to wonder what inversion, displacement, and effacement of history is congealed in this strange proposition, a kind of dream-speak at best, that manifests its profound alliance with what it proclaims to disdain and disavow. Indeed, the entire sequence of papal proclamations on Islam enacted this disavowal and displacement in plain view. It is as if the Pope were saying: "I said it, I did not say it; I cited it; others said it, and so it has authority; this is their aggression, this is my aggression circuited through their aggression, though I have no aggression." The figure through which I name the aggression of Islam is a figure of Christianity's own aggression, at which point the figures converge, and the ability to sustain the distinction between Islam and Christianity founders. Of course, it is that distinction that the Pope seeks to underscore, to make certain, to establish without a shadow of a doubt. But his language upends his argument, starting with the strange way he both appropriates and disavows the citation. The paradox has a social and even psychoanalytic valence, but it seems also to proceed from a certain idea of development and civilizational progress (noting here that one has to distinguish between culture and civilization for all kinds of reasons, but that the latter, despite its origin in the replacement of ecclesiastical authorities by civic courts of law, functions discursively at the present moment to effect a syncretism of religious and secular ideals).

Now it may be in relation to the sorts of arguments described above that we try to make a case for a purely secular resistance. But I am less sure that our ideas of

---

17   "Muhammad's Sword," September 23, 2006, http://zope.gush-shalom.org/home/en/channels/avnery/1159094813/

secularism do not already carry religious content, or that we are, with any of these positions, invoking an unalloyed secularism (it may be that secularism can only be defined by its implication in the very religious traditions from which it seeks to distinguish itself, but that is a broader question toward which I can only gesture in this context). Provisionally, I would suggest that secularism has a variety of forms, many of which involve forms of absolutism and dogmatism that are surely as problematic as those that rely on religious dogma. In fact, a critical perspective does not line up perfectly with the distinction between religious and secular thinking.

The idea of culture in the French instance—a notion of culture that understands itself as "secular"—clearly works in tandem with the papal argument. And though the Pope argues on religious grounds, there are clearly religious opponents to the Pope's views, a situation that suggests we ought not to understand secularism as the sole source of critique, or religion as the sole source of dogmatism. If religion functions as a key matrix for the articulation of values, and if most people in this global condition look to religion to guide their thinking on such matters, we would make a political error in claiming that religion ought to be overcome in each and every instance. Consider that religion is not simply a set of beliefs or a set of dogmatic views, but a matrix for subject formation whose final form is not determined in advance, a discursive matrix for the articulation and disputation of values, and a field of contestation. Similarly, it won't do to embrace secularism as if it were a monolith, since the diversity of secularisms often receive their definition from the nature of the break they make with specific religious inheritances. However, sometimes secularism achieves its definition through the disavowal of a religious tradition that inchoately but continuously informs and supports its own ostensibly post-religious claims. I think the non-contradictory status of the secular Jew, for instance, makes this point explicitly.

We can also see it at work in, for instance, the differential treatment of religious minorities within an ostensibly secular framework, since *laïcité* in France is defined precisely over and against the intrusion of Church authorities into matters of state. The debate on whether girls should be prohibited from wearing the veil in public schools seemed to bring this paradox into relief. The ideas of the secular were invoked to consolidate ignorant and hateful views of Islamic religious practice (i.e., the veil is nothing other than the communication of the idea that women are inferior to men, or the veil communicates an alliance with "fundamentalism"), at which point *laïcité* becomes a way not of negotiating or permitting cultural difference, but of consolidating a set of cultural presumptions that effect the exclusion and abjection of cultural difference.

If I opened this chapter by wondering about the implications of secular progress as a temporal framework for thinking about sexual politics at this time, I would like to suggest now that what is at issue is less any and all ways of looking forward (I hold out for those—I look forward to those!), but an idea of development in which secularism does not so much succeed religion sequentially, as reanimate religion as part of its thesis on culture and civilization. On the one hand, the kind of secularism we are witnessing in France denounces and surpasses the very religious content that it also reanimates in the very terms by which culture is defined. In the case of papal authority, we see a different recourse to a framework, presumptively timeless and binding, that is at once cultural and theological, suggesting an invariable implication of one sphere in the other. These are not quite the same as the idea of Dutch civic integration, but perhaps there are parallelisms, even phantom resonances, that are worth exploring further. The problem is, of course, not progress *per se*, nor surely the future, but specific developmental narratives in which certain exclusionary and persecutory norms become at once the precondition and teleology of culture. Thus, framed both as transcendental condition and as teleology, culture in such instances can only produce a monstrous specter of what lies outside its own framework of temporal thinkability. Outside of its own teleology there exists a ruinous and foreboding sense of the future, and beneath the transcendental condition lurks an aberrant anachronism already broken out upon the political present, sounding the general alarm within the secular frame.

I write this as one trying to come to a critical understanding of, and a political opposition to, the discourse on Islam currently propagated by the US. That leads us to yet another discourse, that of the civilizing mission, and there is not enough space here to try to delineate its logic or to trace its resonance with the other developmental patterns I have been trying to discern in these pages. It is probably worth noting in brief, however, that the US takes its own civilizing mission to involve a crossover of secular and non-secular perspectives. After all, President Bush told us he was guided by God and, for whatever reason, this was the kind of discourse he mobilized at times to rationalize his extra-legal, if not criminal, actions. It would appear that both the secular frame and the civilizational mission, itself only ambiguously secular, are figured as advanced positions that entitle them to bring notions of democracy to those who are characterized as pre-modern, who have not yet entered into the secular terms of the liberal state, and whose notions of religion are invariably considered childish, fanatical, or structured according to ostensibly irrational and primitive taboos. The civilizational mission, as described by Samuel Huntington, is itself a self-avowed mix of religious and secular ideals. Huntington sets forth the notion that the US, representing what he calls somewhat wildly "the West," is considered to have undergone modernization, to have arrived at secular principles that transcend and accommodate religious positions, that are more advanced and finally more rational, and, hence, that it is more capable of democratic deliberation and self-governance.[18] And yet the ideals of democracy Huntington espouses are also those that express the values of a Judeo-Christian tradition, a view that suggests all other religious traditions fall outside the trajectory of modernization that constitutes civilization and its "missionary" claim to the future.

If the Islamic populations destroyed in recent and current wars are considered less than human, or "outside" the cultural conditions for the emergence of the human, then they belong either to a time of cultural infancy or to a time that is outside time as we know it. In both cases, they are regarded as not yet having arrived at the idea of the rational human. It follows from such a viewpoint that the destruction of such populations, their infrastructures, their housing, and their religious and community institutions, constitutes the destruction of what threatens the human, but not of the human itself. It is also precisely this particular conceit of a progressive history that positions "the West" as articulating the paradigmatic principles of the human—of the humans who are worth valuing, whose lives are worth safeguarding, whose lives are precarious, and, when lost, are worth public grieving.

Finally, then, let me offer a final discussion on torture that will take us back to the question of temporality and the rethinking of cultural difference. Let me suggest first that the US relied on a poor anthropological source when it devised its protocols of torture. The Department of Defense assigned a text from the 1970s called *The Arab Mind*, which assumed that there was such a mind, and that it could be characterized in general ways with respect to the religious beliefs and the specific sexual vulnerabilities

---

18   See Samuel Huntington, *The Clash of Civilizations?: The Debate*, London: W.W. Norton & Co. Ltd., 1996; and *Who Are We? The Challenges to America's National Identity*, New York: Simon & Schuster, 2005.

of people of Arab descent.[19] The text subscribed to a form of cultural anthropology that treated cultures as self-sufficient and distinctive, that refused the global mixing of cultural and social formations, and that considered itself beyond moral judgment and more generally in the service of cultural tolerance. I want to suggest that the massive reduction of Arab life to "the Arab mind" produced a ready object for the US military and for the protocols of torture enacted under the direction of General Geoffrey Miller. Since, of course, there is no "Arab mind"—it is not possible to attribute the same fears and anxieties across the Arab world in all its geographical complexity and cosmopolitan formulations—the text had to construct an object that it could then manipulate. Strategies for extracting information from this mind were devised, and they were applied in the various scenes of torture that have become visually available to us, as well as in others that remain unrepresented in any media form.

Those who devised these schemes of torture sought to understand the specific vulnerabilities of a population formed within Islam, and developed their plans as a kind of sexual targeting that was at once a form of religious bigotry or hatred. But what we have to remember is that the subject of Islam was also constructed through the torture, and the anthropological texts—as well as the protocols—were part of the production of that subject within the discourse of the military. I want to be careful here, so let me repeat this formulation: the torture was not merely an effort to find ways to shame and humiliate the prisoners of Abu Ghraib and Guantánamo on the basis of their presumptive cultural formation. The torture was also a way to coercively produce the Arab subject and the Arab mind. That means that regardless of the complex cultural formations of the prisoners, they were compelled to embody the cultural reduction described by the anthropological text.

---

19   See Raphael Patai, *The Arab Mind*, revised edition, Long Island City: Hatherleigh Press, 2002.

Let's remember that the latter does not have an epistemically privileged relation to its subject. It is part of the project to compel the production of that subject, and we will have to ask why.

This perspective has not been considered in the predominant debates on the issue within the mainstream media. There have been, broadly speaking, two ways to approach the issue within a liberal framework. The first presents an argument on the basis of cultural rights and cultural violations. It claims that the orchestrated scenes of sexual and physical humiliation exploit the specific sexual vulnerabilities of these Arab populations. The second position is that one requires a normative condemnation of the torture that makes no reference to culture, since clearly the acts would be wrong and punishable no matter against whom they were perpetrated or who was perpetrating them. The first view, which emphasizes cultural rights, is espoused by the US journalist Seymour Hersh,[20] and maintains that specifically cultural violations occurred in the course of the tortures, violations that had to do with modesty, taboos on homosexuality, and conditions of public exposure and shame. The torture also broke down social codes of sexual difference, forcing men to wear women's lingerie, and debasing women through forced nudity.

Both of these frameworks for understanding the torture are necessary, but are finally insufficient. Yes, there were clearly specific cultural violations at work and these acts of torture were clearly wrong according to any normative framework worth its name; but we have to include both of these views within a larger framework if we are to understand how these scenes of sexual debasement and physical torture are part of the civilizing mission and, in

20   See Seymour Hersh, *The Chain of Command: The Road from 9/11 to Abu Ghraib*, New York: Harper-Collins, 2004; and "The Gray Zone: How a Secret Pentagon Program Came to Abu Ghraib," *New Yorker*, May 25, 2004, http://www.newyorker.com/archive/2004/05/24/040524fa_fact

particular, of its efforts to seize absolute control over the construction of the subject of torture. If we ask what is at stake in producing the Arab subject as a distinctive locus of sexual and social vulnerability, we have to find out what subject position is being staked not only by the US military, but by the war effort more generally. If we want to speak about "specific cultures," then it would make sense to begin with the specific culture of the US army, its emphatic masculinism and homophobia, and ask why it must, for its own purposes, cast the predominantly Islamic population against which it wages war as a site of primitive taboo and shame. I want to suggest that a civilizational war is at work in this context that casts the army as the more sexually progressive culture. The army personnel consider themselves more sexually "advanced" because they read pornography or impose it upon their prisoners, because they overcome their own inhibitions in exploiting and breaking down the inhibitions of those they torture.

The ostensible "superiority" of the army resides not in its capacity to wage war against military subjects, or against the putative sexual and moral codes of Islam, but in its ability to construct the Arab subject coercively through enacting protocols of torture. The point is not simply to break down the codes, but to construct a subject that would break down when coercively forced to break such codes. And I suppose we have to ask: which subject would *not* break down under those conditions? It may be that the torturer postures as one whose impermeability is won at the expense of the radical permeability of the tortured, but that posturing cannot deny a fundamental permeability that traverses all corporeal life. More specifically, for the army to break down those codes is itself an act of domination, but it is also a way of exercising and exemplifying a freedom that is at once lawless and coercive, one that has come to represent and enact the civilizing mission. After all, there can be no civilization with Islam on the "inside," according to the avatars of Huntington and theorists of the so-called "Arab mind." And yet, if we look closely at what is being represented as the civilizing mission, it consists of unbridled homophobic and misogynist practices. Thus, we have to understand the acts of torture as the actions of a homophobic institution against a population that is both constructed and targeted for its own shame about homosexuality; the actions of a misogynist institution against a population in which women are cast in roles bound by codes of honor and shame, and so are not "equal" in the way that women ostensibly are in the West. In this way, we can see the photographs of women without the veil distributed by the US army in Afghanistan as a sign of its "triumph" as prefiguring the digital capture and coerced sexual violation perpetrated by US soldiers in Abu Ghraib and Guantánamo.

In addition, we can see here the association of a certain cultural presumption of progress with a license to engage in unbridled destruction. More specifically, at work in this mode of implicit rationalization is a crude deployment and exploitation of the norm of "freedom" as it operates in contemporary sexual politics, one in which "freedom" becomes not only the means of coercion, but what some might call "the *jouissance* of torture." If we ask what kind of freedom this is, it is one that is free of the law at the same time that it is coercive; it is an extension of the logic that establishes state power—and its mechanisms of violence—as beyond the law. This is not a freedom that belongs to a rights discourse, unless we understand the right to be free of all legal accountability as the right in question.

There are at least two countervailing trends at work in the scenes of torture. On the one hand, the Iraqi prisoner population is considered as pre-modern precisely to the extent that it is understood to embody certain prohibitions and inhibitions in relation to homosexuality, exposure, masturbation, and nudity. The army not only relies upon bad cultural essentialism to make this point, but the torture becomes a way of testing and ratifying the thesis of that bad cultural essentialism. In fact, I would go further: the torture can be understood in this regard as a technique of modernization. Unlike those disciplinary regimes of subject formation that would seek to transform the tortured into exemplary modern subjects, torture of this kind seeks to expose the status of the tortured as the permanent, abased, and aberrant outside of subject-formation as such. If these are subjects of some kind, they are outside the civilizational trajectory that secures the human, which gives the defenders of civilization the "right" to exclude them more violently. Because these are coercive techniques of modernization, however, the question of a barbarity specific to secular modernism is also at stake. And in this regard, we can see that the civilizational mission undertaken by the military in its acts of torture complicates the progressive narrative that would rationalize the war against Islam. We also see in abbreviated form the "deployment" of a position of sexual freedom in order to coerce capitulation to sexual humiliation, at which point the "coercive" dimension of this historical version of the modern secularization project makes itself graphically available. It should be clear that I see the acts of torture neither as aberrant individual acts nor as fully conscious and strategic goals of the US military. Rather, I understand the coercive nature of these acts of humiliation and torture as making explicit a coercion that is already at work in the civilizational mission and, most particularly, in the forced instatement of a cultural order that figures Islam as an abject, backward, foreboding ruination and, accordingly, as requiring subordination within or exclusion from the culture of the human itself. This logic is not far from the disavowal and displacement that marked the Pope's rhetoric on Islam. If Islam is figured as violent by definition, yet encumbered by inhibiting rules, then to the extent that it is violent it requires new disciplinary rules; to the extent that it is rule-bound, it requires an emancipation that only modernity can bring.

I am not claiming that denying someone immigration rights is the same as subjecting that person to sexual torture, but I am suggesting that the rigorous exclusion of Islamic communities from the prevalent norms of Euro-America, to speak broadly for the moment, is based on the conviction that Islam poses a threat to culture, even to prevailing norms of humanization. And when some group of people comes to represent a threat to the cultural conditions of humanization and of citizenship, the rationale for their torture and death is secured— since they can no longer be conceptualized as human or as citizens. In the case of sexual torture, a noxious deployment of the notion of sexual freedom is at work: "we embody that freedom, you do not; therefore, we are free to coerce you, and so to exercise our freedom, and you, you will manifest your unfreedom to us, and that spectacle will serve as the visual justification for our onslaught against you." Of course, this is different from the unveiling of the Afghan women that took place on the front page of the *New York Times*, but is there a common presupposition at work? In these contexts, have feminism and the struggle for sexual freedom become, horrifyingly, a "sign" of the civilizational mission in progress? Can we even begin to understand the torture if we cannot account for the homophobia in the military as it acts on populations who are formed religiously through a taboo on homosexuality?

What kind of encounter is this, then, at the scene of torture, in which a violent homophobia and misogyny exploit the presumptive homophobia and misogyny of its victims? If we focus on the latter, even within a framework of tolerance or cultural rights or specific cultural violations, we lose sight of the precise exploitation at work in the scene of torture. The homophobia and misogyny seem more central to the scene of torture than any homophobia and misogyny that one may have attributed to the tortured population, or indeed that one might understand as the specific liability or backwardness of Islam itself. Whatever the relation is between Islam and the status of women, it is imperative to begin with the proposition that it is complex, historically changing, and not available for a quick reduction (I would suggest that Suad Joseph's edited collection *Women in Islamic Cultures*, four volumes of which have already been published by Brill, might be a good place to start for an English-speaking readership).

What is at issue in the scene of torture is the nexus of violence and sexuality that belongs to the civilizational thesis as it has been formulated in the context of these wars. After all, the US is bringing civilization to the ostensibly "backward" or pre-modern Islamic Other. And what it brings, most clearly, is torture as the instrument and sign of civilization. These are not aberrant moments in the war, but rather the cruel and spectacular logic of US imperial culture as it operates in the context of its current wars. The scenes of torture are conducted in the name of civilization against barbarism, and we can see that the "civilization" at issue is part of a dubious secular politics that is no more enlightened or critical than are the worst forms of dogmatic and restrictive religion. In fact, the historical, rhetorical, and logical alliances between them may be more profound than we think. The barbarism at issue here is the barbarism of the civilizational mission, and any counter-imperialist politics, especially a feminist and queer one, must oppose it at every turn. For the point is to establish a politics that opposes state coercion, and to build a framework within which we can see how the violence done in the name of preserving a certain modernity, and the conceit of cultural homogeneity or integration, form the most serious threats to freedom. If the scenes of torture are the apotheosis of a certain conception of freedom, it is a conception free of all law and free of all constraint, precisely in order to impose law and to exercise coercion. That there are competing notions of freedom at stake is obvious, though it is probably worth noting that the freedom to be protected from coercion and violence is one the meanings that has been lost from view. So, too, is the ability to think time, this time, outside of that teleology that installs itself violently as both origin and end of the culturally thinkable. The possibility of a political framework that opens up our ideas of cultural norms to contestation and dynamism within a global frame would surely be one way to think a politics that re-engages sexual freedom in the context of allied struggles against racism, nationalism, and the persecution of religious minorities.

But I am not at all sure we need to gather those struggles within a unified framework. As I hope I have shown, at least in preliminary form, to insist on a unified cultural framework as a precondition of politics, whether secular or religious, would be to preclude such a framework from political contestation. If, as Marx insists, the point of departure for our analysis must be the historical present, then it seems to me that a new way of understanding how temporalities conflict and converge will be necessary for any complex description of that present. This means, I think, resisting both unified frameworks that would distill the antagonisms in question into equivalent rights claims, but also refusing those developmental narratives that would determine in advance what a just view of human flourishing consists in. It is always possible to show not only the various ways in which Islam is modern but also, just as importantly, how certain secular ideals could not have been developed without their transmission and elaboration through Islamic practices. The point, however, is not to show that we are all modern. If modernity seeks to constitute itself through a continuous and unfolding idea of time, and if some of our personal liberties are conceptualized within that notion of a continuous and unfolding realization, then perhaps we would do well to remember Nietzsche's quip from *The Will to Power*: "Mankind does not advance, it does not even exist."[21]

---

21   Friedrich Nietzsche, *The Will to Power*, ed. W. Kaufman, trans. W. Kaufman and R. J. Hollingdale, New York: Vintage, 1968.

More salient, perhaps, is Walter Benjamin's insistence, in
the thirteenth of his *Theses on the Philosophy of History*, "that
the concept of the historical progress of mankind cannot
be sundered from the concept of its progression through
a homogeneous, empty time. A critique of the concept of
such a progression must be the basis of any criticism of
the concept of progress itself."[22] He notes in a subsequent
thesis that "the awareness that they are about to make
the continuum of history explode is characteristic of the
revolutionary classes at the moment of their action."[23] The
historian who understands how the past flashes up, how
the past is not past, but continues in the present, is one
who understands "the time of the now" as "shot through
with chips of Messianic time."[24] Benjamin's emphatically
non-secular reference here does not rely on an ideal future
to come, but rather on the interruptive force of the past on
a present that effaces all qualitative differences through its
homogenizing effect. The "constellation" which is one's
own era is precisely the difficult and interruptive scene of
multiple temporalities that cannot be reduced to cultural
pluralism or a liberal discourse of rights. For Benjamin,
in the final line of those theses, "every second of time was
the strait gate through which the Messiah might enter,"
an historical condition under which political responsibility
for the present exists precisely "now." It is not by accident
that Benjamin understood the revolutionary action as
the strike, as the rejection of coercive state power. That
power relies on a certain taken-for-granted notion of
historical progress to legitimate itself as the ultimately
modern achievement. To separate the "now time" from
these claims of modernity is to undercut the temporal
framework that uncritically supports state power, its

---

22   Walter Benjamin, *Illuminations*, ed. H. Arendt, trans. H. Zohn, New York:
Schocken Books, 1968.
23   Ibid., 261.
24   Ibid., 263.

legitimating effect, and its coercive instrumentalities. Without a critique of state violence and the power it wields to construct the subject of cultural difference, our claims to freedom risk an appropriation by the state that can make us lose sight of all our other commitments. Only through such a critique of state violence do we stand a chance of finding and acknowledging already existing alliances and sites of contact with other minorities in order to consider systemically how coercion seeks to divide us and to keep attention deflected from the critique of violence itself.

It is only by coming to terms with the epistemic shifts among critical perspectives, both secular and religious, that any of us will be able to take stock of the time and place of politics. If freedom is one of the ideals we hope for, it will be important to remember how easily the rhetoric of freedom can be deployed in the name of the self-legitimation of a state whose coercive force gives the lie to its claim to safeguard humanity. Maybe then we can rethink freedom, even freedom from coercion, as a condition of solidarity among minorities, and appreciate how necessary it is to formulate sexual politics in the context of a pervasive critique of war.

4

Non-Thinking in the Name of the Normative

In a recent exchange,[1] the British sociologist Chetan Bhatt remarked that "in sociology, cultural theory or cultural studies, many of us assume a field of truths ... a (albeit contested) field of theoretical intelligibility for understanding or describing 'Self', 'Other', the subject, identity, culture."[2] He adds: "I am no longer sure these concepts necessarily have the expansive capacity to speak to the massive transformations of life-worlds outside Euro America, the rapid unscrambling and repackaging of what we call 'identity' ..." If Bhatt is right, then the very framework by which we proceed, whether that of multiculturalism or human rights, presumes specific kinds of subjects that may or may not correspond to the

---

1   *British Journal of Sociology* 59: 1 (2008). My essay, "Sexual Politics, Torture, and Secular Time," appearing in revised form as Chapter 3 of the present volume, was originally given as the annual lecture for the *British Journal of Sociology* in October 2007 at the London School of Economics. It was first published in the *BJS* along with several responses. This chapter is a revised and expanded version of the rejoinder I offered to those responses ("A Response to Ali, Beckford, Bhatt, Modood and Woodhead," in *British Journal of Sociology* 59: 2, 255–60) and includes a discussion of Talal Asad's work that did not appear in those pages.

2   Chetan Bhatt, "The Times of Movements: A Response," *British Journal of Sociology*, 59: 1 (2008), 29.

modes of life in play within the present time. The subjects presumed by the liberal and multicultural frameworks (and we will have to try to distinguish between them) are characterized as belonging to certain kinds of cultural identities, variously conceived as singularly or multiply determined by lists of categories that include ethnicity, class, race, religion, sexuality, and gender. There are persistent questions about whether and how such subjects can be represented in law, and what might count as sufficient cultural and institutional recognition for such subjects. We ask such normative questions as if we know what we mean by the subject even as we do not always know how best to represent or recognize various subjects. Indeed, the "we" who asks such questions for the most part assumes that the problem is a normative one, namely, how best to arrange political life so that recognition and representation can take place. And though surely this is a crucial, if not the most crucial, normative question to ask, we cannot possibly approach an answer if we do not consider the ontology of the subject whose recognition and representation is at issue. Moreover, any inquiry into that ontology requires that we consider another level at which the normative operates, namely, through norms that produce the idea of the human who is worthy of recognition and representation at all. That is to say, we cannot ask and answer the more commonly understood normative question, regarding how best to represent or to recognize such subjects, if we fail to understand the differential of power at work that distinguishes between those subjects who will be eligible for recognition and those who will not. In other words, what is the norm according to which the subject is produced who then becomes the presumptive "ground" of normative debate?

The problem is not merely or only "ontological" since the forms the subject takes as well as the life-worlds that do not conform to available categories of the subject emerge in light of historical and geopolitical movements. I write that they "emerge" but that is, of course, not to be taken for granted, since such new formations can "emerge" only when there are frames that establish the possibility for that emergence. Thus, the question is: are there such frames and, if so, how do they work? There are variants on liberalism and multiculturalism which propose to think about what recognition might be in light of the challenge to notions of the subject and identity proposed by Bhatt above. Some of these positions seek to extend a doctrine of recognition to coalitional subjects. Sociologist Tariq Modood, for example, proposes a conception of citizenship relying less on subject-based perspectives or claims than on the inter-subjective exchange that takes place, for instance, as a result of "coalitional possibilities between sexual politics and religious multiculturalism." In his view, citizenship has to be understood as dynamic and revisable, as marked by "conversations and re-negotiations." A substantial conception of citizenship implies modes of dialogue that reconstitute the participants in significant ways. Modood makes clear that "the one thing that civic inclusion does not consist of is an uncritical acceptance of an existing conception of citizenship, of 'the rules of the game' and a one-sided 'fitting-in' of new entrants or the new equals (the ex-subordinates)." He then makes this important addition to his remarks: "To be a citizen, no less than to have just become a citizen, is to have a right to not just be recognized but to debate the terms of recognition."[3]

Making the demand to become a citizen is no easy task, but debating the terms by which that citizenship is conferred is surely even more difficult. In this perspective, the citizen *is itself* a coalitional exchange; in other words, there is no singly or multiply determined subject, but a

---

3   Tariq Modood, "A Basis for and Two Obstacles in the Way of a Multiculturalist Tradition," *British Journal of Sociology*, 59: 1 (2008), 49; see also Modood, *Multiculturalism: A Civic Idea*, London: Polity, 2007, and Sara Ahmed, Claudia Casteneda, Anne-Marie Fortier, and Mimi Sheller, eds., *Uprootings/Regroundings: Questions of Home and Migration*, London: Berg Publishers, 2003.

dynamic social process, a subject who is not only under way, but constituted and reconstituted in the course of social exchange. One is not only entitled to a certain status as a citizen, but this status is itself determined and revised in the course of social interaction. We might say that this dialogic form of social ontology is all well and good, but that legal recognition makes juridical subjects of us all. Although that may well be true, there are extra-legal conditions for becoming a citizen, indeed, for even becoming a subject who can appear before the law. To appear before the law means that one has entered into the realm of appearance or that one is positioned to be entered there, which means that there are norms that condition and orchestrate the subject who can and does appear. The subject who is crafted to appear before the law is thus not fully determined by the law, and this extra-legal condition of legalization is implicitly (non-juridically) presupposed by law itself.

We might be tempted then to resolve on formulating a new conception of the subject, one that might be termed "coalitional." But what will constitute the parts of the coalition? Shall we say that there are several subjects within a single subject, or that there are "parts" that enter into communication with one another? Both alternatives beg the question of whether the language of the subject suffices. Consider the scenario invoked by those who pursue the normative goal of tolerance: if one subject exercises tolerance toward another, or two different subjects are enjoined to exercise tolerance reciprocally, then these two subjects are considered differentiated from the start. But what accounts for that differentiation? And what if "differentiation" is precisely what must be repressed and relocated in order for the subject to appear within such a scenario? Posited within some discourses of tolerance, for instance, are two different kinds of subjects, such as "homosexuals" and "Muslims," who either do or do not tolerate each other in the spheres of public transaction and policy. As Wendy Brown has persuasively argued, tolerance is a weak instrument, often presupposing a disdain for those toward whom it is directed.[4] Others favor recognition as a more robust and affirmative alternative to tolerance (less tolerant, and so more tolerant!). But recognition becomes a less than perspicacious concept when we think about how it might work in relation to such scenarios. Apart from the question of who confers recognition and what form it takes, we also have to ask what is it precisely that would be "recognized"? Is it the "homosexuality" of the gay person? Is it the religious belief of the Muslim? If our normative frameworks presuppose that these ostensibly defining features of singly determined subjects are its proper objects, then recognition becomes part of the very practice of ordering and regulating subjects according to pre-established norms. If recognition reconsolidates the "sexual subject," the "cultural subject," and the "religious subject," among others, does it *make* or *find* the subject of recognition, and is there any way of distinguishing between making and finding within the scene of recognition based on such terms? What if the very features that are "recognizable" prove to rely on a failure of recognition?

The fact that no subject can emerge without being differentiated has several consequences. In the first instance, a subject only becomes discrete through excluding other possible subject formations, a host of "not-me's." In the second instance, a subject emerges through a process of abjection, jettisoning those dimensions of oneself that fail to conform to the discrete figures yielded by the norm of the human subject. The refuse of such a process includes various forms of spectrality and monstrosity, usually figured in relation to non-human animal life. In

---

4   See Wendy Brown, "Tolerance as Supplement: The 'Jewish Question' and the 'Woman Question'," in *Regulating Aversion: Tolerance in the Age of Identity and Empire*, Princeton, NJ: Princeton University Press, 2006, 48–77.

a way, this formulation is a kind of (post)structuralist truism in the sense that difference not only preconditions the assertion of identity, but proves as a result to be more fundamental than identity. Laclau and Mouffe offered their extremely important reformulation of this notion in *Hegemony and Socialist Strategy*, where it would seem that the condition of differentiation becomes at once the sign of a constitutive lack in all subject formation and a basis for a non-substantial conception of solidarity.[5]

Is there a way of turning this set of formal insights into a historically specific analysis of the differential working of recognition in these times? After all, if the subject is always differentiated, we have to understand precisely what that means. We tend to understand differentiation both as an internal feature of a subject (the subject is internally differentiated and composed of several mutually determining parts) and as an external feature (the subject excludes other formations of the subject as well as specters of abjection or the loss of subject status). But these two forms of differentiation are not as distinct as they might appear, since the one I exclude in order to constitute my discreteness and specificity remains internal to me as the prospect of my own dissolution. Any internal differentiation I might make between my parts or my "identities" relies upon some way of unifying those differences, and so re-installs the subject as the ground of difference itself. In turn, this subject gains its specificity by defining itself against what is outside itself, and so the external differentiation proves to be central to the account of internal differentiation as well.

One need go no further than Hegel to make such points, but perhaps there is something more to be considered in the specific forms that ostensible cultural conflicts take, as

---

5   Ernesto Laclau and Chantal Mouffe, *Hegemony and Socialist Strategy: Towards a Radical Democratic Politics*, London: Verso, 1985. See also Simon Critchley and Oliver Marchart, eds., *Laclau: A Critical Reader*, London: Routledge, 2004.

well as in the way those forms are presupposed by prevalent normative frameworks. The homosexual person at issue may or may not be Muslim, and the Muslim person at issue may or may not be homophobic. But if the framework of cultural conflict (gay versus Muslim) determines how we conceive of those identities, then the Muslim becomes defined by his or her ostensible homophobia, and the homosexual becomes defined, depending on the framework, either as presumptively anti-Muslim or fearful of Muslim homophobia. In other words, both positions get defined in terms of their putatively conflictual relation with one another, at which point we come to know very little about either category or the sites of their sociological convergence. Indeed, the framework of tolerance, even the injunction to tolerance, orders identity according to its requirements and effaces the complex cultural realities of gay and religious lives.

The consequence is that the normative framework mandates a certain ignorance about the "subjects" at issue, and even rationalizes this ignorance as necessary to the possibility of making strong normative judgments. Indeed, it takes some effort to "understand" the cultural realities designated by "homosexual" and "Muslim," especially in their transnational "life-worlds," to invoke Bhatt, both inside, outside, and at the periphery of Euro-America (understanding that these spatial categories can operate simultaneously). After all, to understand this relation would involve considering a number of formations in which sexuality and religion operate as vehicles for one another, sometimes in antagonism, and sometimes not. To say that there are rules against homosexuality within Islam is not yet to say how people live in relation to such rules or taboos, or how such rules and taboos vary in their intensity or centrality, depending on the specific religious contexts and practices at issue. Especially of interest would be an analysis of how sexual practices explicitly tabooed take place in relation to the taboo, or in relative indifference to it. To say that there is a taboo at a doctrinal level is not yet to explain what function the taboo has within that doctrine and how sexual lives are conducted in relation not only to the taboo itself, but to several other kinds of cultural realities, whether religiously inflected or not. Indeed, even to say that religion and sexuality may both constitute driving forces for a way of life is still not to say how much of a drive they might be, or in what ways they drive (or fail to drive), or what precisely it is that they drive (and in tandem with what other driving forces?). In other words, the binary framework assumes that religion and sexuality are both singly and exhaustively determining of identity (which is why there are two identities, distinct and opposed). Such a framework fails to consider that even where there are antagonisms, that does not imply contradiction or impasse as necessary conclusions. Antagonism can be lived within and among subjects as a dynamic and productive political force. Finally, such a framework does not bother to ask about the complex ways that religion and sexuality are organized, since the binary framework assumes to know all that it needs to know prior to any actual investigation of this complex cultural reality It is a form of non-thinking ratified by a restrictively normative model, one that wants a map of reality that can secure judgment even if the map is clearly false. Indeed, it is a form of judgment that falsifies the world in order to shore up moral judgment itself as the sign of a certain cultural privilege and "perspicacity"—a way of keeping the hordes at bay (which would presumably not only include non-Europeans, but also comparativists of all kinds). And such claims often go along with a spurious assertion of "political courage," understood as the willingness to defy those who would have us think about cultural differences in more grounded, patient, or complex ways. In other words, we do not need to understand, but only and always to judge! My point, though, is not to paralyze judgment or to undermine normative claims, but to insist that we must devise new constellations for thinking about normativity if we are to proceed in intellectually open and comprehensive ways to grasp and evaluate our world.

There are, of course, some options that I am *not* promoting. For instance, the problem we are addressing is not one in which the rights of culture threaten to trump rights of individual freedom, since that framing of the problem refuses to rethink the very concepts of the individual and of culture being presumed. In this context, it is important to emphasize that the effort of secular elites to exclude religion from the public sphere may be rooted in a certain class privilege and blindness to the fact that religious networks often provide the support on which vulnerable populations necessarily rely. Some have made the case for the associational rights of religious communities on the grounds that the infringement of such rights leads to substantive disenfranchisement for such communities or, indeed, the deracination of community itself.[6] Of course, such a project would have to be able to locate communities, to treat them as stable and discrete entities, and this would lead to some complicated sorts of decisions about how group membership is to be determined. Indeed, the advantage of such an approach is that it supplements a certain individualism through a notion of group rights; but the limitation is that the "group" or the "community" functions as a unified subject precisely at a time in which new social formations require that we think beyond or against such assumed unities.

The strategy of devising associational rights and a coalitional concept of citizenship might be understood to expand existing democratic norms in ways that make them more inclusive, and that may overcome the "stand-offs" between individual and religious claims and rights. Doubtless, such strategies have their strengths and

---

6   See Linda Woodhead, "Secular Privilege, Religious Disadvantage," in *British Journal of Sociology*, 59: 1 (2008), 53–8.

promise. I wish only to draw attention to the tension between (a) expanding the existing normative concepts of citizenship, recognition, and rights to accommodate and overcome contemporary impasses, and (b) the call for alternative vocabularies grounded in the conviction that the normative discourses derived from liberalism and multiculturalism alike are inadequate to the task of grasping both new subject formations and new forms of social and political antagonism.

Although I would be loath to underestimate the place of social and cultural conflict in contemporary politics, I would be equally reluctant to take "impasse" for granted as a structural feature of multiculturalism, however prevalent the construal of a certain "stand-off" between, for instance, religious and sexual minorities may be. There are numerous religious gay and lesbian groups, some of which have been responsible for some of the pro-marriage agendas in the US.[7] There are existing coalitions of queers and "illegal aliens" or *sans papiers* in the US and across Europe that work together without conflicts over sexual identity and religious belief affecting their coalitional efforts. And there are numerous networks of Muslim lesbians and gays (consider the Kreuzberg bar, SO36, in Berlin) that undo the necessity of the opposition between sexuality and religion. If we consider how their HIV status has adversely effected the ability of certain individuals to migrate or, indeed, to attain adequate health care, we can see how communities struggling for enfranchisement, characterized by a fusion of

---

7   Consider a few of the organizations that represent Muslims and Arab sexual minorities: Imaan, an organization in the UK for gay, lesbian, bisexual, and transgendered Muslim people, offering social services and community outreach: www.imaan.org.uk. See also www.al-bab.com, a website offering various resources for Arab lesbian and gay people, some of which have a religious content while others do not. See also "The International Initiative for the Visibility of Queer Muslims," queerjihad.blogspot.com, and www.al-fatiha. org, an international organization for lesbian, gay, bisexual, and transgender Muslims.

identities, may be formed under the rubric of immigration politics. If the terms of multiculturalism and the politics of recognition require either the reduction of the subject to a single, defining attribute, or the construction of a multiply determined subject, then I am not sure we have yet faced the challenge to cultural metaphysics posed by new global networks that traverse and animate several dynamic determinations at once.

When such networks form the basis of political coalitions, they are bound together less by matters of "identity" or commonly accepted terms of recognition than by forms of political opposition to certain state and other regulatory policies that effect exclusions, abjections, partially or fully suspended citizenship, subordination, debasement, and the like. In this sense, "coalitions" are not necessarily based on subject positions or on reconciling differences among subject positions; indeed, they can be based on provisionally overlapping aims and there can be—perhaps must be—active antagonisms over what these aims should be and how best to reach them. They are animated fields of differences, in the sense that "to be effected by another" and "to effect another" are part of the very social ontology of the subject, at which point "the subject" is less a discrete substance than an active and transitive set of interrelations.

I am not at all convinced that there is one "unifying" term to cover all the forms of dispossession that link minority politics, nor do I think there need be one for the strategic purposes of political alliance. What is necessary is that those engaged in such coalitional efforts be actively involved in thinking through the category of the "minority" as it crosses the lines that divide citizen from non-citizen. By focusing on state and regulatory powers, how they orchestrate debate and manipulate the terms for creating a political impasse, we move beyond the kind of framework that presumes a dyadic opposition or that extracts a "conflict" from a complex formation in such a way that occludes the coercive and orchestrating dimensions of normative frames. By bringing the question of power to the center, the terms of the debate are bound to change and, indeed, to become more politically responsive.

So, how do forms of power, including state power, orchestrate a scene of dyadic opposition, requiring two discrete subjects, qualified by single or plural attributes, and mutually exclusive? To take such subjects for granted is to deflect critical attention from the operations of power itself, including the orchestrating effects of power in and on subject formation. As a consequence, I caution against narrative forms of progressive history in which either dyadic conflict is overcome through more encompassing and inclusive liberal frameworks, or else in which the conceit of progress itself becomes the defining issue in the battle to defend liberalism. In the first case, we develop more inclusive frameworks to solve the antagonism; in the second, we claim that the secular and progressive alternative is the *sine qua non* of liberal democracy and declare effective war on any effort to rethink or challenge the necessity, sufficiency, and ultimate value of that alternative. The first characterizes dialectical, pragmatist, and progressive notions of history; the second makes the "progressive" into one pole of a conflict and casts as threats to liberalism all non-secular and counter-progressivist vocabularies, including all efforts to develop alternative vocabularies for thinking about emergent subjects and effective languages, media, and idioms for political enfranchisement.

I certainly do not imagine a "seamless" alliance between religious and sexual minorities. There are existing alliances, and it makes sense to ask how they are formed. It also makes sense to assume that they will contain within them certain fractures, failures, and continuing antagonisms. By saying "contain within them," I do not mean to suggest that the alliance sutures or resolves such antagonisms. On the contrary, with Laclau and Mouffe, I would continue to argue that antagonism keeps the alliance open and suspends the idea of reconciliation as a goal. What might keep an alliance together is different from the question of what keeps an alliance mobile. What keeps an alliance mobile is, in my view, the continued focus on those formations of power that exceed the strict definition of identity applied to those included in the alliance. In this case, an alliance would need to stay focused on methods of state coercion (ranging from immigration tests to explicit torture) and on the invocations (and reductions) of the *subject, nature, culture, and religion* that produce the ontological horizon within which state coercion appears necessary and justified.

The operation of state power takes place within an ontological horizon saturated by power that precedes and exceeds state power. As a result, we cannot take account of power if we always place the state at the center of its operation. The state draws upon non-statist operations of power and cannot function without a reserve of power that it has not itself organized. Further—and this is not particularly new—the state both produces and presupposes certain operations of power that work primarily through establishing a set of "ontological givens." Among those givens are precisely notions of subject, culture, identity, and religion whose versions remain uncontested and incontestable within particular normative frameworks. So when we speak about "frameworks" in this respect, we are not simply talking about theoretical perspectives that we bring to the analysis of politics, but about modes of intelligibility that further the workings of the state and, as such, are themselves exercises of power even as they exceed the specific domain of state power.

Perhaps the most salient site where an "impasse" emerges is not between the minority sexual subject and the minority religious subject, but between a normative framework that requires and produces such subjects in mutual conflict and a critical perspective that questions whether and how such subjects exist outside—or in various relations to—that presumptive antagonism. This would imply a consideration of how that framework depends upon and induces a refusal to understand the complexity of the historical emergence of religious/sexual populations and subject formations that cannot be reduced to either identity form. On the one hand, it is possible to say that such reductions, however falsifying, are necessary because they make possible normative judgments within an established and knowable framework. The desire for epistemological certainty and certain judgment thus produces a set of ontological commitments that may or may not be true, but which are deemed necessary in order to hold firm to existing epistemological and ethical norms. On the other hand, the practice of critique, as well as the practice of providing a more adequate historical understanding, focus on the violence effected by the normative framework itself, thus offering an alternative account of normativity based less on ready judgment than on the sorts of comparative evaluative conclusions that can be reached through the practice of critical understanding. Indeed, how do we reapproach the politics of judgment and evaluation once we begin to think critically and comparatively about competing schemes of evaluation?

In order to broach this last question, I want to return to Talal Asad's recent book, *On Suicide Bombing*, which I considered briefly in Chapter 1.[8] This may seem like a surprising move since Asad makes it clear that his own work is "not an argument" but, rather, an attempt at "understanding"—he explicitly refuses to decide on the matter of what kind of violence is justified and what is not. At first glance, Asad would seem to offer a point of view that directly conflicts with those who would maintain the necessity of moral judgment even when, or precisely when, they maintain ignorance of the cultural practices they judge. Asad argues in favor of understanding. He does so, I want to suggest, precisely in order to destabilize and

8   Asad, *On Suicide Bombing*.

rework our conceptions of what normativity is, and in that way he makes a distinct contribution to normative theory.

Asad makes very clear that he is attempting to provide an understanding of "suicide bombing" as it is constructed and elaborated within "Western public discourse." He remarks that he is not in the business of elaborating moral judgment, even though he insists, in a repeated and significant aside, that he does not approve of suicide bombing tactics.[9] He wants, however, for the purposes of his analysis, to set aside that kind of judgment in order to ask and to pursue other kinds of questions. In a similar vein, he is not interested in reconstructing the motivations of suicide bombers, though I have no doubt he would agree that such a study might furnish interesting results. Given that he is restricting himself to the analysis of what, perhaps over-broadly, he terms "Western" public discourse on suicide bombing, how are we to understand this self-restriction? Are we to take him at his word when he tells us that normative judgments are not at work in the "understanding" of the phenomenon that he seeks to provide? Over and against Asad's explicit claims, I want to reintroduce some of the normative questions that are set aside in his book. But I do this not to prove the book wrong or misguided, only to suggest that there is a stronger normative position here—a more consequential exploration of normativity—than its author explicitly allows.

My question, then: can we find a way of rethinking the terms of normativity by virtue of the kind of account Asad gives? At first one might feel justified, if not righteous, in demanding that Asad make more clear where he stands: can he offer an analysis of suicide bombing that does not ultimately lead to a conclusion about whether it is a justified form of violence? If we pose this question too quickly, we may well miss the chance to understand what he is trying to tell us about the question itself. To be clear:

---

9   Ibid., 4.

he is offering no justification for suicide bombings, and neither is he dwelling on the normative arguments against them. He is, I want to suggest, standing to the side of the "for and against" arguments in order to change the framework in which we think about these kinds of events or, rather, to understand how such phenomena are seized upon by certain moral and cultural frameworks and instrumentalized for the purposes of strengthening the hold of those frameworks on our thinking. In the preface to the Japanese edition of *On Suicide Bombing,* Asad writes:

> I examine the arguments that try to distinguish the terror of modern warfare from the terror inflicted by militants, arguments whose main thrust is to claim a moral superiority for 'just' war and to describe the acts of terrorists—and especially the suicide bombers—as uniquely evil. My argument is that the fundamental difference is merely one of scale, and that by this criterion the state-directed destruction of civilians and the disruption of their normal life is far greater than anything terrorists can do.[10]

Another instance in which Asad distances himself from the question of justification in order to open up the possibility of a different sort of evaluative claim occurs in his review of Michael Walzer's position on just wars.[11] For Walzer, wars in defense of a community are justified when that community is (a) threatened with elimination, or (b) subject to a coercive transformation of its way of life. Walzer also reviews the reasons why states ought to go to war and explores a set of justificatory arguments for engaging in violence. His enumeration of possible justifications makes assumptions about what any justification might be,

---

10   Text cited courtesy of Talal Asad.
11   Asad, *On Suicide Bombing,* 14–24. See also Michael Walzer, *Just and Unjust Wars,* New York: Basic Books, 1992; and *Arguing About War,* New Haven: Yale University, 2004. The latter is the focus of Asad's extended critique.

circumscribing in advance the domain in which it makes sense to debate justifications at all. Walzer's point is not that some forms of violence are justified and others not (although this is a point he will also make), but that we can only rightly debate whether or not certain forms of violence are justified if we restrict ourselves to those kinds of violence he has already delimited: state violence for the purposes of just wars; that is, the defense of the "community," when the community in question is recognizable according to established and familiar norms of recognition. Apparently, there are other forms of violence that are not worth debating, and for which we are not expected to supply reasons for their justification.

What Walzer calls "terrorism" is one such instance, and he warns against any efforts to explain or justify this phenomenon.[12] As we know, "terrorist" can apply variously and wildly to both insurgency and counter-insurgency groups, to state and non-state sponsored violence, to those who call for more fully democratic forms of government in the Middle East, and even to those who criticize the repressive measures of the US government. Given this semantic sliding, it seems all the more necessary to take the time to clarify what precise meaning the term is meant to convey. Without knowing precisely what we are speaking about, how are we to understand the strong normative judgments that follow with regard to the term "terrorism"? For Walzer, "terrorist violence" falls outside the parameters of both justified and unjustified violence. To distinguish between the latter we must consider

---

12 Note the resonance with Walzer's infamously anti-intellectual response after 9/11, when he argued that we should make no room for those who seek to understand the reasons for the attacks on the US. Calling those who would offer such analyses "excuseniks," he cast a curious aspersion, likening those who might seek to understand the events with "refuseniks"—the dissidents who opposed the censorious practices of the Soviet Union. The term is currently used to describe those young Israelis who refuse to be conscripted into the Israeli army on moral or political grounds.

whether the forms of violence in question conform to the normative requirements Walzer has laid out, but so-called "terrorist" violence, as he conceives it, falls outside of the purview of this debate. Since Walzer's scheme thus refuses to consider the reasons given for certain kinds of violence, especially when they are considered simply "evil," what he calls "terrorist violence" forms the constitutive outside for those forms of violence that might reasonably be debated. The form of violence his scheme puts outside of reflection and debate is patently unreasonable and non-debatable. But for whom is this true? And what does this tell us about the kinds of restricted normative vocabularies that form the uncritical precondition for Walzer's own reflections?

Asad points out that Walzer's condemnation of terrorism follows from his definition of it, and that that definition could easily prove to be too inclusive. Walzer writes that the evil of terrorism consists "not only in the killing of innocent people but also the intrusion of fear into everyday life, the violation of private purposes, the insecurity of public spaces, the endless coerciveness of precaution."[13] Is there any reason to think that all of these consequences do not also follow from state-sponsored wars? Asad focuses on the stipulative definition of terrorism in Walzer's work in order to show how such definitions not only carry normative force, but also effectively—and without justification—make normative distinctions. Asad writes:

> I am not interested here in the question, "When are particular acts of violence to be condemned as evil, and what are the moral limits to justified counter-violence." I am trying to think instead about the following question: "What does the adoption of particular definitions of death dealing do to military conduct in the world?"[14]

13   Asad, *On Suicide Bombing*, 16.
14   Ibid., 20.

Asad's point is that the definitions at work circumscribe the means of justification. So, if state killing is justified by military necessity, then any and all sorts of state killing can be justified by this norm, including those that kill innocents, introduce fear into everyday life, violate private purposes, render public spaces insecure, and produce infinitely coercive precautionary measures. We can indeed think about the wars in Iraq and Afghanistan along with their domestic repercussions in all of these ways, as we can also about most of the wars launched by the US and its allies during the past decades.

In any event, this takes us back to the question of whether there is a stronger normative dimension to this kind of inquiry than its author explicitly allows. If Asad sets aside the question of whether or not a form of violence is justified, it is not because he has some particular sympathy for that violence, but because he is interested in showing us how the domain of justifiability is preemptively circumscribed by the definition of the form of violence at issue. In other words, we think of definitions as purely heuristic and as preceding the matter of judging. We define the phenomenon so that we know what we are talking about, and then we submit the phenomenon to judgment. Conventionally, the first task is descriptive, and the second is normative. But if the very definition of the phenomenon involves a description of it as "evil," then the judgment is built into the definition (we are, in fact, judging before knowing), at which point the distinction between the descriptive and the normative becomes confused. Moreover, we have to ask whether the definition is right, since it may well consist of a conceptual elaboration of the phenomenon that takes place without any descriptive reference. Indeed, it may well be that definition has been substituted for description, and that both are, in fact, judgments—at which point judgment, and the normative, have preempted the descriptive altogether.

We judge a world we refuse to know, and our judgment becomes one means of refusing to know that world.

The point is not to insist upon a neutral description of the phenomenon, but rather to consider how a phenomenon like "terrorism" becomes defined in ways that are vague and overly inclusive. Most importantly, though, if we were to try to take stock of the different forms of violence that emerge within contemporary life, how might our normative distinctions be altered, and how would we compare and contrast these forms of violence? Would they be as distinct as Walzer claims they are? And if they were not so distinct, what would follow? Would we have to devise new criteria and new forms of judgment? And which vocabulary—or set of vocabularies—would have to be available for those new judgments to emerge?

If we begin with the assumption that justified violence will be undertaken by certain kinds of states (those generally regarded as embodying principles of liberal democracy) or certain kinds of communities (those where the population's cultural and material life is already valued and explicitly represented by liberal democracies), then we have already built a certain political demographics into the definition of what might qualify as justified violence. In other words, concrete assumptions will already have been made about the kinds of populations whose lives— and modes of life—are worth defending by military means. If, however, we open up those very demographic distinctions to critical analysis, then we have to ask how it is that our conception of violence, in both its justified and unjustified forms, has built into it certain pre-conceptions about what culture ought to be, about how community is to be understood, about how the state is formed, and about who might count as a recognizable subject. Here we can see that some of the very terms through which contemporary global conflicts are conceptualized dispose us in advance towards certain kinds of moral responses and normative conclusions. What follows from this analysis is not that there ought to be no conclusions, but only that our conclusions need to be based upon a field of description and understanding that is both comparative and critical in character.

It may be that Asad opens up some questions for us when, for instance, he asks about the ways in which "terrorism" is defined, but if one looks closely at the questions he poses, it turns out that they make sense only on condition that reference is made to a horizon of comparative judgment. So, although Asad himself claims that his book "makes no case for accepting some kinds of cruelty as opposed to others," but seeks merely to "disturb" the reader and produce some critical distance from a "complacent public discourse," much more is actually at stake.[15] I assume that we are not being asked simply to stay in a state of "disturbance" and "distance" from ready-made moral reactions. To take distance from the "ready-made" is precisely a critical activity.

Further, when Asad asks how we are to conceive of death-dealing at this time, and whether state-sponsored wars disrupt everyday life any more or less than do "terrorist" acts, he effectively points out that once we are able to think comparatively about these forms of violence—which means understanding them as part of a contemporary spectrum of death-dealing—we will see that the disruptions and invasions caused by state violence far exceed those caused by acts falling under the category of "terrorist." If this is the case, and if we can only arrive at this comparative judgment through an understanding of scale, then part of the critical project of Asad's work is precisely to make this scale of violence available for subsequent judgments—something that cannot be done when, prior to any comparative analysis, we ratify certain epistemic commitments that bias our understanding of "state violence" as a precondition for justifiable violence.

---

15   Ibid., 5.

If Asad's analysis shows us that state violence can and does produce all the "evil" consequences that Walzer attributes to "terrorism"—and if, further, we understand those consequences to be truly lamentable and unjust—then it follows that any condemnation of violence will logically extend to forms of state violence that produce those same consequences.

Asad's argument is presented as an attempt to reveal the self-contradiction or hypocrisy inherent in positions such as Walzer's, but I would argue that Asad's own position derives its rhetorical force from a political opposition to forms of violence that intrude on everyday life, deracinate infrastructures, produce unacceptable levels of fear, and involve relentless coercion. It is only on the condition that we do, in fact, oppose such forms of violence that we can come to understand the normative importance of the comparative judgment Asad's work makes available to us. I would suggest, then, that it is not the case that Asad's work merely opens up new avenues for description or understanding while eschewing the hard work of moral judgment. On the contrary, by exposing the ways in which normative dispositions enter into stipulative claims that circumscribe the domain of "understanding," Asad provides us with the tools to develop a critique of this parochial circumscription, and offers a new framework by which to make comparative judgments, leading us to the conclusion that there is no reason to assume that justified violence is the sole prerogative of states while unjustified violence is exercised only by illegitimate states and insurgency movements. To refer to the violence committed by an "insurgency" is already to invoke another framework, even though it does not by itself resolve the question of whether or not that violence is justified. For the US, yesterday's "terrorists" have a way of becoming tomorrow's "freedom fighters," and vice versa (*nota bene*: Nicaragua, Afghanistan). The point is not to conclude that cynicism is the only option, but to consider more closely the conditions and terms under which such inversions of discourse take place, in order, finally, to make better judgments.

In concluding his book Asad poses again the question with which he began: "why do people in the West react to verbal and visual representations of suicide bombing with professions of horror?"[16] In asking the question, he is assuming that powerful affective responses are conditioned and structured by interpretations, and that these interpretations are formed within taken-for-granted frameworks, largely Western and liberal. These interpretive structures remain inchoate when we take "moral affect"—including horror and indignation—to be so many emotive emanations of the universal human that supposedly resides in us all. The fact is that "horror" and "outrage" are differentially distributed, and what is worth noting—with surprise and a different register of horror—is how this differential distribution remains so often unremarked and unmarked. The point is not to dispute the nascent intelligence of "horror" as an affective response, but only to ask about those occasions in which horror becomes the predominant reaction in contrast with those other encounters with violence in which horror is clearly and emphatically absent.[17] What are the social conditions and abiding interpretative frameworks that make horror possible in the face of certain kinds of violence, and when and where is it "ruled out" as an available affective response in the face of other kinds?

Asad offers a complex argument about the liberal constituents of identity, suggesting that suicide bombing strikes at what holds the liberal subject together, asking whether "suicide terrorism (like a suicidal nuclear strike) belongs in this sense to liberalism?" One of "the tensions

---

16   Ibid., 65.
17   For an interesting account of contemporary horror, see Adriana Cavarero, *Horrorism: Naming Contemporary Violence*, New York: Columbia University Press, 2008.

that hold modern subjectivity together" involves two apparently opposite values: "reverence for human life and its legitimate destruction." Under what conditions does that reverence become primary? And under what conditions is that reverence abrogated through recourse to precepts of just wars and legitimate violence? Asad remarks, "Liberalism, of course, disapproves of the violent exercise of freedom outside the frame of law. But the law is founded by and continuously depends on coercive violence." This paradoxical founding of political liberalism makes itself known in the "tensions that hold modern subjectivity" in what Asad calls "the West."[18]

In fact, these tensions expose the rifts in modern subjectivity, but what is particularly modern is the vacillation between these two principles that are split off from one another, forming something like a dissociative disorder at the level of political subjectivity. Paradoxically, what holds the subject together for Asad is the capacity to shift suddenly from one principle (reverence for life) to another (legitimate destruction of life) without ever taking stock of the reasons for such a shift and for the implicit interpretations that condition these distinct responses. One reason we want to know about such apparently inexplicable shifts is that they appear to form the moral groundwork for an acceptable political subjectivity, which is to say that an unreasoned schism functions at the basis of this contemporary political rationality.

I would like to suggest that what Asad offers us is a critique of a certain kind of liberal subject that makes that very subject into a political problem to be explicitly addressed. We can take this subject as the ground of politics only if we agree not to think well or carefully about the conditions of its formation, its moral responses, and its evaluative claims. Let us recall the kind of fundamental claims that are made in the course of "normative" debate

---

18   Ibid., 65.

about these issues; for example, that there are "subjects," Muslim or homosexual, who stand in positions of moral opposition to one another; that they represent different "cultures" or different "times in historical development," or fail to conform to established notions of "culture" or intelligible conceptions of "time," as the case may be. One response to this framework is to insist that there are different constructions of the subject at work, and that most versions of multiculturalism err when they assume that they know in advance what the form of the subject must be. The multiculturalism that requires a certain kind of subject actually institutes that conceptual requirement as part of its description and diagnosis. What formations of subjectivity, what configurations of life-worlds, are effaced or occluded by such a mandatory move?

Sociologists such as Chetan Bhatt draw attention to the complex and dynamic character of new global subject-formations, which would include the crossing of gay and Muslim identities, the production of alliances among the legally disenfranchised, and the migratory constitution of dynamic subject positions that do not reduce to single identities. Bhatt's conceptualization attempts to produce an alternative vocabulary for thinking about the subject; in a sense, Asad addresses this problem from the opposite direction. Taking as his point of departure the political subject instituted through liberalism, Asad shows how its moral responses and evaluative schemes are culturally specific and politically consequential precisely at that moment when its parochialism passes itself off as universal reason. Taken together, these positions offer at least two good reasons not to treat a specific form of the subject, or the reduction of the subject to identity, as a taken-for-granted feature of normative frameworks: the risk of anachronism and the risk of mandating parochialism as universality. Such arguments do not destroy the basis of normative reasoning, but they do raise normative questions about how that form of reasoning has been preemptively circumscribed. It is important to argue that there are normative reasons for opposing this move on the part of prevalent normative frameworks. The point, again, is not to dispense with normativity, but to insist that normative inquiry take on a critical and comparative form so that it does not unwittingly reproduce the internal schisms and blind spots inherent to those versions of the subject. These internal schisms become the unjustifiable ground (actually, the failure of any ground) for the unjust judgment that certain lives are worth saving and others worth killing. In this sense, it is under the aegis of equality and toward a greater egalitarianism that Asad's criticism takes place.

My last point is that coalition itself requires a rethinking of the subject as a dynamic set of social relations. Mobilizing alliances do not necessarily form between established and recognizable subjects, and neither do they depend on the brokering of identitarian claims. Instead, they may well be instigated by criticisms of arbitrary violence, the circumscription of the public sphere, the differential of powers enacted through prevalent notions of "culture," and the instrumentalization of rights claims for resisting coercion and enfranchisement. Whether we expand our existing frameworks or allow them to be interrupted by new vocabularies will determine, in part, how well we consult both the past and the future for our present-day critical practices.

If we take for granted the theoretical field of multiculturalism that assumes distinct subjects with opposing points of view, then the solution to the problem is one in which we find domains of compatibility or incompatibility. We expand our notions of rights to include everyone, or we work to construct more robust notions of recognition that will allow for some kind of reciprocal relationship and future harmony. But that very theoretical field is based on a set of foreclosures (and here I use the term outside of its regular Lacanian meaning). As a result, we confront a certain rift or schism that recurs at the heart of contemporary politics. If certain lives are deemed worth living, protecting, and grieving and others not, then this way of differentiating lives cannot be understood as a problem of identity or even of the subject. It is rather a question of how power forms the field in which subjects become possible at all or, rather, how they become impossible. And this involves a critical practice of thinking that refuses to take for granted that framework of identitarian struggle which assumes that subjects already exist, that they occupy a common public space, and that their differences might be reconciled if only we had the right tools for bringing them together. The matter is, in my view, more dire and requires a kind of analysis capable of calling into question the framework that silences the question of who counts as a "who"—in other words, the forcible action of the norm on circumscribing a grievable life.

5

The Claim of Non-Violence

I doubt very much that non-violence can be a principle, if by "principle" we mean a strong rule that can be applied with the same confidence and in the same way to any and all situations. If there is a claim of non-violence or if non-violence makes a claim upon us, that seems to be a different issue. Non-violence then arrives as an address or an appeal. The pertinent question then becomes: under what conditions are we responsive to such a claim, what makes it possible to accept the claim when it arrives, or, rather, what provides for the arrival of the claim at all?

The capacity to respond to the claim has everything to do with how the claim is formed and framed, but also with the disposition of the senses, or the conditions of receptivity itself. Indeed, the one who responds is crafted forcibly by norms that often do a certain kind of violence, and may well dispose that subject towards a certain kind of violence as well. So violence is not foreign to the one to whom the address of non-violence is directed; violence is not, at the start, presumptively "outside." Violence and non-violence are not only strategies or tactics, but form the subject and become its constitutive possibilities and, so, an ongoing struggle. To say this is to suggest that non-violence is the struggle of a single subject, but also that the norms that act upon the subject are social in nature, and the bonds that are at stake in the practice of non-violence are social bonds. Thus, the singular "one" who struggles with non-violence is in the process of avowing its own social ontology. Though debates on this topic often presume we can separate with ease the matters of individual practice and of group behavior, perhaps the challenge of non-violence is precisely a challenge to the presumption of such dual ontologies. After all, if the "I" is formed through the action of social norms, and invariably in relation to constitutive social bonds, then it follows that every form of individuality is a social determination. Conversely, every group is not only delimited from another, but composed of a differentiated assemblage, which presumes that singularization constitutes an essential feature of sociality.

The problem, however, cannot be definitively answered through recourse to such arguments, even though they are, in my view, crucial to any critical consideration of non-violence. We have to ask "non-violence against whom?" and "non-violence against what?" There are distinctions to be made, for instance, between violence against persons, against sentient beings, against property, or against the environment. Moreover, there are forms of violence that are meant to counter or to stop other violence: the tactics of self-defense, but also the violence enacted in the name of combating atrocity or famine or other humanitarian crises, or in revolutionary efforts to institute a democratic politics. Although in this brief, final chapter I cannot address these crucial issues in their specificity and urgency, I can perhaps sketch more broadly the conditions of possibility for registering the claim of non-violence. Who is the subject to whom the address of non-violence is directed, and through what frames is that claim made sensible? There may be any number of decisions to be made once the claim is registered (one may well register and resist the claim), but my wager is that if there is responsiveness to the claim, then it will become less easy to accept violence as a taken-for-granted social fact.

In a recent exchange in *differences*, I was asked by the philosopher Catherine Mills to consider an apparent paradox.[1] Mills points out that there is a violence through which the subject is formed, and that the norms that found the subject are by definition violent. She asks how, then, if this is the case, I can make a call for non-violence. We might pause right away and ask whether it is only norms that form the subject, and whether the norms that do take part in that formation are necessarily violent. But let's accept the thesis for the moment, and see where it leads.

We are at least partially formed through violence. We are given genders or social categories, against our will, and these categories confer intelligibility or recognizability, which means that they also communicate what the social risks of unintelligibility or partial intelligibility might be. But even if this is true, and I think it is, it should still be possible to claim that a certain crucial breakage can take place between the violence by which we are formed and the violence with which, once formed, we conduct ourselves. Indeed, it may be that precisely because one is formed through violence, the responsibility not to repeat the violence of one's formation is all the more pressing and important. We may well be formed within a matrix of power, but that does not mean we need loyally or automatically reconstitute that matrix throughout the course of our lives. To understand this, we have to think for a moment about what it is to be formed and, in particular, to be formed by norms, and whether that forming happens once, in the past, or in a way that is unilinear and effective. Such norms act productively to establish (or disestablish) certain kinds of subjects, not only in the past but also in a way that is reiterated through time. Norms do not act only once. Indeed, it is

---

1   "Violence and Non-Violence of Norms: Reply to Mills and Jenkins," *differences* 18: 2 (2007). Portions of this chapter are drawn from this response.

not possible to narrate the beginning of the action of such norms, although we can, fictionally, posit such a beginning, often with great interest—and we can also, I suppose, try to locate the place and time when a certain formation was said to be accomplished (though I would wager that such a chronology is invariably constructed in bad faith). If gender, for instance, acts on us "in the beginning," it does not then cease to act upon us, and the primary impressions are not ones that begin and end in time. Rather, they are ones that establish the temporality of our lives as bound up with the continuing action of norms, the continuing action of the past in the present, and so the impossibility of marking the origin and end of a gender formation as such. We do not need to refer to two distinct temporal events, that is, to claim that at a given point in time there are normative conditions by which subjects are produced and then afterwards, at another point in time, there are "breaks" with such conditions. The normative production of the subject is an iterable process—the norm is repeated, and in this sense is constantly "breaking" with the contexts delimited as the "conditions of production."

The idea of iterability is crucial for understanding why norms do not act in deterministic ways. And it may also be the reason why performativity is finally a more useful term than "construction."[2] Even if we were able to describe the "origin" of norms and to offer a description outside of a fictional rendition, what use would it be? If the aims of a norm cannot be derived from its origins (as Nietzsche clearly tells us, for instance, with regard to legal conventions), then even if norms originated in violence it would not follow that their fate is only and always to

---

2   Performative effects may well be (or become) material effects and are part of the very process of materialization. Debates on construction tend to become mired in the question of what is not constructed and so seem bound up with a metaphysics they are supposed to avoid. Performativity may, in the end, entail a shift from metaphysics to ontology and offer an account of ontological effects that allows us to rethink materiality itself.

reiterate the violence at their origin. And it would also still be possible that, if norms do continue to exercise violence, they do not always do so in the same way. Moreover, it would have to be shown that the violence at the origin is the same as the violence exercised in the iterations that produce the norm through time.

Does the origin of the norm constrain all future operations of the norm? It may well function to establish a certain control over temporality, but does another temporality—or do several—emerge in the course of its iterations? Is this at least a possibility, something that one might try to orchestrate or call for? What one is pressing for, calling for, is not a sudden break with the entirety of a past in the name of a radically new future. The "break" is nothing other than a series of significant shifts that follow from the iterable structure of the norm. To say that the norm is iterable is precisely not to accept a structuralist account of the norm, but to affirm something about the continuing life of poststructuralism, a preoccupation with notions such as *living on, carrying on, carrying over, continuing*, that form the temporal tasks of the body.

All that said, I would caution against a generalization of the thesis that all normativity is founded in violence. This kind of claim can function as a transcendental argument and so fail to distinguish those social instances when norms operate for other reasons, or when the term "violence" does not quite describe the power or force by which they operate. There are, to be sure, regimes of power that produce and constrain certain ways of being. But I am not at all sure about affirming or denying a transcendental thesis that would dismiss power from the equation and make violence essential to any and all subject formation.[3]

---

3   For a further consideration of this issue, see my "Violence, Non-Violence: Sartre on Fanon," in *The Graduate Faculty Philosophy Journal* 27: 1 (2006), 3–24; and Jonathan Judaken, ed., *Race after Sartre: Antiracism, Africana Existentialism, Postcolonialism*, Albany: SUNY Press, 2008, 211–32.

An ethical proscription against the waging of violence does not disavow or refuse that violence that may be at work in the production of the subject. In fact, to understand a call to non-violence, it is probably necessary to reverse the formulation altogether: when one is formed in violence (and here the "one" may be formed through national structures of bellicosity that take various tributary forms in civil and private life), and that formative action continues throughout one's life, an ethical quandary arises about how to live the violence of one's formative history, how to effect shifts and reversals in its iteration. Precisely because iterability evades every determinism, we are left with questions such as: How do I live the violence of my formation? How does it live on in me? How does it carry me, in spite of me, even as I carry it? And in the name of what new value can I reverse and contest it? In what sense can such violence be redirected, if it can? Precisely because iterability evades every voluntarism, I am not free to dispense with the history of my formation. I can only live on in the wake of this unwilled region of history, or, indeed, *as* its wake. Can one work with such formative violence against certain violent outcomes and thus undergo a shift in the iteration of violence? Perhaps the better word here is "aggression" or, less clinically, "rage," since my view is that non-violence, when and where it exists, involves an aggressive vigilance over aggression's tendency to emerge as violence. As such, non-violence is a struggle, forming one of the ethical tasks of clinical psychoanalysis and of the psychoanalytic critique of culture.

Indeed, non-violence as an ethical "call" could not be understood if it were not for the violence involved in the making and sustaining of the subject. There would be no struggle, no obligation, and no difficulty. The point is not to eradicate the conditions of one's own production, but only to assume responsibility for living a life that contests the determining power of that production; in other words, that makes good use of the iterability of the productive norms and, hence, of their fragility and transformability. The social conditions of my existence are never fully willed by me, and there is no agency apart from such conditions and their unwilled effects. Necessary and interdependent relations to those I never chose, and even to those I never knew, form the condition of whatever agency might be mine. And though not all unwilled effects are "violent," some of them are impingements that are injurious, acting forcibly on the body in ways that provoke rage. This is what constitutes the dynamic bind or "struggle" that is non-violence. It has, I would submit, nothing to do with cleansing or expiating violence from the domain of normativity, nor does it involve finding and cultivating an ostensibly non-violent region of the soul and learning how to live according to its dictates.[4] It is precisely because one is mired in violence that the struggle exists and that the possibility of non-violence emerges. Being mired in violence means that even as the struggle is thick, difficult, impeding, fitful, and necessary, it is not the same as a determinism—being mired is the condition of possibility for the struggle for non-violence, and that is also why the struggle so often fails. If this were not the case, there would be no struggle at all, but only repression and the quest for a false transcendence.

Non-violence is precisely neither a virtue nor a position and certainly not a set of principles that are to be applied universally. It denotes the mired and conflicted position of a subject who is injured, rageful, disposed to violent retribution and nevertheless struggles against that action (often crafting the rage against itself). The struggle against violence accepts that violence is one's own possibility. If that acceptance were not there, if one postured rather as a beautiful soul, as someone by definition without violent

---

4   See Mahatma Gandhi's writings on non-violence in which the practice is precisely not a quiescent one. *Mahatma Gandhi: Selected Political Writings*, ed. Dennis Dalton, Indianapolis: Hackett Publishing, 1996.

aggression, there could be no ethical quandary, no struggle, and no problem. Such a position of virtue or principle of purity would disavow or repress the violence from which such positions are wrought. It is crucial to distinguish between (a) that injured and rageful subject who gives moral legitimacy to rageful and injurious conduct, thus transmuting aggression into virtue, and (b) that injured and rageful subject who nevertheless seeks to limit the injury that she or he causes, and can do so only through an active struggle with and against aggression. The first involves a moralization of the subject that disavows the violence it inflicts, while the latter necessitates a moral struggle with the idea of non-violence in the midst of an encounter with social violence as well as with one's own aggression (where the social encounter and the "one's own" transitively affect one another). This last accepts the impurity of the subject and the unwilled dimension of social relations (which includes elements of those relations that are explicitly willed), and accepts as well that the prospects for aggression pervade social life. The struggle to which I refer becomes heightened precisely when one has been subject to aggression and injured, and when the desire for retribution is sharpened. This may be a personal struggle, but the parameters of that struggle clearly pervade political situations of conflict in which the move to retribution is made quickly and with full moral certitude. It is this juncture of violence and moralization I am trying to undo by suggesting that responsibility may well find a different mooring.

For Levinas, violence is one "temptation" that a subject may feel in the encounter with the precarious life of the other that is communicated through the face. This is why the face is at once a temptation to kill and an interdiction against killing. The "face" would make no sense if there were no murderous impulse against which it had to be defended. And its very defenselessness is what apparently stokes the aggression against which the interdiction functions. Levinas has articulated a certain ambivalence for the subject in the encounter with the face: a desire to kill, an ethical necessity not to kill.[5]

For Melanie Klein, this ambivalence takes on another form. Her speculations on murderous rage follow from her analysis of mourning and loss.[6] For Klein, the relation to the "object" is one of annihilation and preservation. Introjection is the mode by which a lost object is "preserved," but that melancholic solution can lead to destructive consequences. Klein attributes a consuming aggression to the subject who suffers loss; the "other" who is lost is psychically "consumed" through a kind of introjective cannibalism. The other installed within the psyche continues to be "berated" internally, and so, according to Klein, a critical voice emerges that comes to characterize "moral sadism."[7] This moral sadism is resonant with the moralization of violence that I mentioned above. The other who is lost becomes incorporated (as a way of preserving that other), but is also berated (not only for "going away" but as a consequence of the general ambivalence of love relations). Thus, the melancholic solution restructures the ego in precisely such a way that the lost other is incessantly preserved and incessantly destroyed, without either process reaching a final conclusion. The rage felt against the other and against the loss of that other constitutes a reflexive turn that constitutes the surviving subject's self-annihilating soliloquy. Something preserving has to get in the way of this self-annihilating tendency, but the suicidal risk is that the ego will, in Klein's terms, seek to preserve

---

5   See my discussion of Levinas and the prohibition against killing in the final chapter of *Precarious Life*. References to Levinas in this chapter are to Emmanuel Levinas, "Peace and Proximity," *Basic Philosophical Writings*, Adriaan T. Peperzak, Simon Critchley, and Robert Bernasconi, eds., Bloomington, W: Indiana University Press, 1966, 161–9.
6   Klein, "A Contribution to the Psychogenesis of Manic-Depressive States," 115–46.
7   Ibid., 122–3.

the other, the ideal of the other, at the expense of itself—
that the one who is dead or gone will still potentially be
perceived as having been destroyed by the surviving self,
such that, paradoxically, the only way to save the lost other
at the expense of one's own life.

What is important to note here is that the ambivalence
Klein describes in relation to melancholia is generalizable
to the conditions of love and attachment in general. For
Klein, melancholia internalizes an object that sets up a
scene of persecution, creating an unsurvivable situation for
the ego and precipitating the expulsion of internal objects,
often without regard for whether they are, in Klein's sense,
"good" or "bad." In "Mourning and Melancholia" Freud
traced the super-ego's function to the internalization and
transformation of the lost other as a recriminating voice, a
voice that spoke precisely what the ego would have spoken
to the other had the other remained alive to hear the
admonitions of the one who was left.[8] The criticisms and
recriminations addressed to the absent other are deflected
and transformed into an internal voice directed against the
self. Recrimination that remains unspeakable against the
other becomes finally speakable only against the self, which
ends up being a way of saving the other, even in death, from
one's own accusatory voice. Turned back upon oneself to
"save the life of the other," one's own voice becomes the
instrument of one's own potential annihilation. The result
is that for the ego to live, it must let the other die, but
that proves difficult when "letting die" feels too close to
"murder" or, indeed, to taking impossible responsibility
for the other's death. Better to take one's own life than
become a murderer, even if taking one's life confirms
oneself as a murderer of the self. Who needs Althusser
or the police when the raging speech of the melancholic
himself wields the power of self-annihilation? The police do

8   Sigmund Freud, *Mourning and Melancholia* (1917), trans. James Strachey,
Standard Edition, 14: 243–58, London: Hogarth Press, 1957.

not have to hail the melancholic for his or her own voice to level an acute accusation. The difference between a livable conscience and an unlivable one is that self-murder, in the former case, remains partial, sublimated, and faulty; it fails to become either suicide or murder, which is to say that, paradoxically, only a faulty conscience stands a chance of countering destructive violence.

Klein takes this scenario of the heightened super-ego in melancholia and recasts it as psychic servitude, describing at length "the slavery to which the ego submits when complying with the extremely cruel demands and admonitions of its loved object which has become installed within the ego." She continues: "these strict demands serve the purpose of supporting the ego in its fight against its uncontrollable hatred and its bad attacking objects, with whom the ego is partially identified."[9] Significantly, the moralization of the voice as "cruel demands and admonitions" precipitates the formation of the super-ego. The super-ego is not erected primarily as a restraint upon libidinal desire, but rather as the circuitry that appropriates and defers primary aggression and its annihilating consequences. The super-ego thus supports the ego in its fight against its own "uncontrollable hatred." By marshalling its own aggression against itself, the ego is moved in the direction of a perilous self-sacrifice.

Luckily, this is not a closed system and certainly not a foundational ontology for the subject, since this very economy can and does change. As a sign of the instability internal to the economy, annihilation motivates the subject but so too does preservation. Like Levinas, Klein refers to an "anxiety" about the well-being of the object. Since this subject was ambivalent from the start, it can occupy that conflict in a different way. In relation to the object (living or dead), the self (ego) feels anxiety and remorse as well as "a sense of responsibility," protecting itself against

9   Klein, "The Psychogenesis of Manic-Depressive States," 123.

persecutors who are psychic figures for the ego's own destructive impulses, and protecting those it loves against its own persecutions. Indeed, persecution is distributed in fragments, signifying the break-up of the object (through aggression) and the return of that destruction in dismembered form.[10] Klein thus refers to the psychic scene as one in which each fragment of the disintegrated object grows again into a persecutor. The ego is not merely frightened of the specter of fragmentation it has produced; it also feels sadness toward the object, responds to the impending loss of the object, a loss that it can, may, or will institute as a consequence of its own destructiveness.

As I pointed out in Chapter 1, guilt, for Klein, seeks to ward off the prospect of unsurvivable loss. Its "moralization" is secondary, even a deflection, and if there is any morality at work here, it consists solely in the insight that the "I" needs the other in order to survive, that the "I" is invariably relational, that it comes into being not only through a sustaining, but through the formation of a capacity to sustain an address to another. This is a point which, another time, would lead us to consider the important transition from Klein to Winnicott. For Winnicott, the question is whether the object of love can survive our love, can bear a certain mutilation and still persist as an object.[11] But for Klein, the effort to preserve the object against our own destructiveness reduces finally to a fear for one's own survival.

For both of these positions, so obviously opposed, destructiveness forms the problem for the subject. Even if aggression is coextensive with being human (and implicitly

---

10   "The ego then finds itself confronted with the psychical fact that its loved objects are in a state of dissolution—in bits—and the despair, remorse and anxiety deriving from this recognition are at the bottom of numerous anxiety situations." "The Psychogenesis of Manic-Depressive States," 125.

11   D. W. Winnicott, "Transitional Objects and Transitional Phenomena," *International Journal of Psychoanalysis* 34 (1953 [1951]), 89–97. See also *Playing and Reality*, London: Tavistock Publications Ltd, 1971.

undoes the anthropocentric understanding of the human animal), the way that destructiveness is lived and directed varies enormously. Indeed, it can become the basis of a "non-moralized" sense of responsibility, one that seeks to protect the other against destruction. This is precisely the alternative to moral sadism, a violence that righteously grounds itself in an ethics of purity wrought from the disavowal of violence. It is also the alternative to the ontologization of violence considered to be so structurally fixed and deterministic at the level of the subject that it precludes any possibility of an ethical commitment to safeguard the life of another.

Here we can see an important distinction between moral sadism and responsibility. Whereas moral sadism is a mode of persecution that passes itself off as virtue, responsibility in the above sense "owns" aggression as well as the ethical mandate to find a non-violent solution to rageful demands. It does this not in obedience to a formal law, but precisely because it seeks to protect the other against its own destructive potential. In the name of preserving the precarious life of the other, one crafts aggression into modes of expression that protect those one loves. Aggression thus restricts its violent permutation, subordinating itself to that claim of love that seeks to honor and protect the precarious life of the other. For Klein, as well as for Levinas, the meaning of responsibility is bound up with an anxiety that remains open, that does not settle an ambivalence through disavowal, but rather gives rise to a certain ethical practice, itself experimental, that seeks to preserve life better than it destroys it. It is not a principle of non-violence, but a practice, fully fallible, of trying to attend to the precariousness of life, checking the transmutation of life into non-life.

It is precisely within an ongoing contestation over power that the question of doing or not doing violence emerges. It is not a position of the privileged alone to decide whether violence is the best course; it is, paradoxically, even painfully, also the obligation of the dispossessed to decide whether to strike back and, if so, in what form. In the face of massive state violence, for example, it may well seem foolish or extraneous to pose the question; but it also may be that, under some circumstances, the non-reciprocated violent act does more to expose the unilateral brutality of the state than any other. I'm not sure non-violence saves the purity of anyone's soul, but it does avow a social bond, even when it is violently assaulted from elsewhere.

State violence often articulates itself through the positing of the sovereign subject. The sovereign subject poses as precisely not the one who is impinged upon by others, precisely not the one whose permanent and irreversible injurability forms the condition and horizon of its actions. Such a sovereign position not only denies its own constitutive injurability but tries to relocate injurability in the other as an effect of doing injury to that other and exposing that other as, by definition, injurable. If the violent act is, among other things, a way of relocating the capacity to be violated (always) elsewhere, it produces the appearance that the subject who enacts violence is impermeable to violence. The accomplishment of this appearance becomes one aim of violence; one locates injurability with the other by injuring the other and then taking the sign of injury as the truth of the other. The specific moralization of this scene takes place when the violence is "justified" as "legitimate" and even "virtuous," even though its primary purpose is to secure an impossible effect of mastery, inviolability, and impermeability through destructive means.

To avow injurability does not in any way guarantee a politics of non-violence. But what may well make a difference would be the consideration of precarious life, and so too injurability, as a generalized condition, rather than as a differential way of marking a cultural identity, that is, a recurrent or timeless feature of a cultural subject who is persecuted or injured by definition and irregardless of historical circumstance. In the first instance, the "subject" proves to be counter-productive for understanding a shared condition of precariousness and interdependency. In the second instance, the "subject" is re-installed and becomes defined by its injury (past) and injurability (present and future).[12] If a particular subject considers her- or himself to be by definition injured or indeed persecuted, then whatever acts of violence such a subject commits cannot register as "doing injury," since the subject who does them is, by definition, precluded from doing anything but suffering injury. As a result, the production of the subject on the basis of its injured status then produces a permanent ground for legitimating (and disavowing) its own violent actions. As much as the sovereign subject disavows his injurability, relocating it in the other as a permanent repository, so the persecuted subject can disavow his own violent acts, since no empirical act can refute the *a priori* presumption of victimization.

If non-violence has the opportunity to emerge here, it would take its departure not from a recognition of the injurability of all peoples (however true that might be), but from an understanding of the possibilities of one's own violent actions in relation to those lives to which one is bound, including those whom one never chose and never knew, and so those whose relation to me precedes the stipulations of contract. Those others make a claim upon me, but what are the conditions under which I can hear or respond to their claims? It is not enough to say, in Levinasian vein, that the claim is made upon me prior to my knowing and as an inaugurating instance of my coming into being. That may be formally true, but its truth is of no use to me if I lack the conditions for responsiveness that allow me to apprehend it in the midst of this social and political life. Those "conditions"

---

12   I am continually indebted here, as elsewhere, to "Wounded Attachments," Chapter 3 of Wendy Brown's *States of Injury: Power and Freedom in Late Modernity*, Princeton, NJ: Princeton University Press, 1995.

include not just my private resources, but the various mediating forms and frames that make responsiveness possible. In other words, the claim upon me takes place, when it takes place, through the senses, which are crafted in part through various forms of media: the social organization of sound and voice, of image and text, of tactility and smell. If the claim of the other upon me is to reach me, it must be mediated in some way, which means that our very capacity to respond with non-violence (to act against a certain violent act, or to defer to the "non-act" in the face of violent provocation) depends upon the frames by which the world is given and by which the domain of appearance is circumscribed. The claim to non-violence does not merely interpellate me as an individual person who must decide one way or another. If the claim is registered, it reveals me less as an "ego" than as a being bound up with others in inextricable and irreversible ways, existing in a generalized condition of precariousness and interdependency, affectively driven and crafted by those whose effects on me I never chose. The injunction to non-violence always presupposes that there is some field of beings in relation to whom non-violence ought to be the appropriate bearing. Because that field is invariably circumscribed, non-violence can only make its appeal by differentiating between those against whom violence ought not to be waged and those who are simply "not covered" by the injunction itself.

For the injunction to non-violence to make sense, it is first necessary to overcome the presumption of this very differential—a schematic and non-theorized inegalitarianism—that operates throughout perceptual life. If the injunction to non-violence is to avoid becoming meaningless, it must be allied with a critical intervention apropos the norms that differentiate between those lives that count as livable and grievable and those that do not. Only on the condition that lives are grievable (construed within the future anterior) does the call to non-violence avoid complicity with forms of epistemic inegalitarianism. The desire to commit violence is thus always attended by the anxiety of having violence returned, since all the potential actors in the scene are equally vulnerable. Even when such an insight follows from a calculation of the consequences of a violent act, it testifies to an ontological interrelation that is prior to any calculation. Precariousness is not the effect of a certain strategy, but the generalized condition for any strategy whatsoever. A certain apprehension of equality thus follows from this invariably shared condition, one that is most difficult to hold fast in thought: non-violence is derived from the apprehension of equality in the midst of precariousness.

For this purpose, we do not need to know in advance what "a life" will be, but only to find and support those modes of representation and appearance that allow the claim of life to be made and heard (in this way, media and survival are linked). Ethics is less a calculation than something that follows from being addressed and addressable in sustainable ways, which means, at a global level, there can be no ethics without a sustained practice of translation—between languages, but also between forms of media.[13] The ethical question of whether or not to do violence emerges only in relation to the "you" who figures as the potential object of my injury. But if there is no "you," or the "you" cannot be heard or seen, then there is no ethical relation. One can lose the "you" through the exclusive postures of sovereignty and persecution alike, especially when neither admits to being implicated in the position of the other. Indeed, one effect of such modes of sovereignty is precisely to "lose the you."

Non-violence thus would seem to require a struggle over the domain of appearance and the senses, asking how best

---

13   See Sandra Bermann, Michael Wood, and Emily Apter, eds., *Nation, Language, and the Ethics of Translation*, Princeton, NJ: Princeton University Press, 2005.

to organize media in order to overcome the differential ways through which grievability is allocated and a life is regarded as a life worth living or, indeed, as a living life. It is also to struggle against those notions of the political subject that assume that permeability and injurability can be monopolized at one site and fully refused at another. No subject has a monopoly on "being persecuted" or "being persecuting," even when thickly sedimented histories (densely compounded forms of iteration) have produced that ontological effect. If no claim to radical impermeability is finally acceptable as true, then no claim to radical persecutability is finally acceptable either. To call into question this frame by which injurability is falsely and unequally distributed is precisely to call into question one of the dominant frames sustaining the current wars in Iraq and Afghanistan, but also in the Middle East. The claim of non-violence not only requires that the conditions are in place for the claim to be heard and registered (there can be no "claim" without its mode of presentation), but that anger and rage also find a way of articulating that claim in a way that might be registered by others. In this sense, non-violence is not a peaceful state, but a social and political struggle to make rage articulate and effective—the carefully crafted "fuck you."

In effect, one has to come up against violence to practice non-violence (they are bound together, and tensely so); but, it bears repeating, the violence one is up against does not issue exclusively from the outside. What we call aggression and rage can move in the direction of nullifying the other; but if who we "are" is precisely a shared precariousness, then we risk our own nullification. This happens not because we are discrete subjects calculating in relation to one another, but because, prior to any calculation, we are already constituted through ties that bind and unbind in specific and consequential ways. Ontologically, the forming and un-forming of such bonds is prior to any question of the subject and is, in fact, the social and affective condition of subjectivity. It is also a condition that installs a dynamic ambivalence at the heart of psychic life. To say that we have "needs" is thus to say that who we "are" involves an invariable and reiterated struggle of dependency and separation, and does not merely designate a stage of childhood to be surmounted. It is not just "one's own" struggle or the apparent struggle of "another" but precisely the dehiscence at the basis of the "we," the condition under which we are passionately bound together: ragefully, desirously, murderously, lovingly.

To walk the line is, yes, to live the line, the impasse of rage and fear, and to find a mode of conduct that does not seek to resolve the anxiety of that position too quickly through a decision. It is, of course, fine to decide on non-violence, but decision cannot finally be the ground for the struggle for non-violence. Decision fortifies the deciding "I," sometimes at the expense of relationality itself. So the problem is not really about how the subject should act, but about what a refusal to act might look like when it issues from the apprehension of a generalized condition of precariousness or, in other words, of the radically egalitarian character of grievability. Even the "refusal to act" does not quite capture the forms of stalled action or stoppage that can, for instance, constitute the non-violent operation of the strike. There are other ways of conceiving the blocking of those reiterated actions that reproduce the taken-for-granted effects of war in daily life. To paralyze the infrastructure that allows armies to reproduce themselves is a matter of dismantling military machinery as well as resisting conscription. When the norms of violence are reiterated without end and without interruption, non-violence seeks to stop the iteration or to redirect it in ways that counter its driving aims. When that iteration continues in the name of "progress," civilizational or otherwise, it makes sense to heed Walter Benjamin's trenchant remark that "Perhaps revolutions are nothing other than human beings on the train of progress reaching for the emergency brake."[14]

To reach for the brake is an "act," but it is one that seeks to forestall the apparent inexorability of a reiterated set of acts that postures as the motor of history itself. Maybe the "act" in its singularity and heroism is overrated: it loses sight of the iterable process in which a critical intervention is needed, and it can become the very means by which the "subject" is produced at the expense of a relational social ontology. Of course, relationality is no utopian term, but a framework (the work of a new frame) for the consideration of those affects invariably articulated within the political field: fear and rage, desire and loss, love and hatred, to name a few. All this is just another way of saying that it is most difficult when in a state of pain to stay responsive to the equal claim of the other for shelter, for conditions of livability and grievability. And yet, this vexed domain is the site of a necessary struggle, a struggle to stay responsive to a vicissitude of equality that is enormously difficult to affirm, that has yet to be theorized by the defenders of egalitarianism, and that figures in a fugitive way in the affective and perceptual dimensions of theory. Under such circumstances, when acting reproduces the subject at the expense of another, not to act is, after all, a way of comporting oneself so as to break with the closed circle of reflexivity, a way of ceding to the ties that bind and unbind, a way of registering and demanding equality affectively. It is even a mode of resistance, especially when it refuses and breaks the frames by which war is wrought time and again.

---

14   Walter Benjamin, *Gesammelte Werke*, Frankfurt: Suhrkamp Verlag, I: 1232. See also my "Critique, Coercion, and Sacred Life in Benjamin's 'Critique of Violence'," in *Political Theologies*, ed. Hent de Vries, New York: Fordham University Press, 2006, 201–19.

Index